The Wonderful Name of Jesus

By

E.W. KENYON

Jesus wants to take away the guilt, fear, condemnation & that comes from sin.

ISBN 1-57770-007-4

Twenty-Eighth Printing

CONTENTS

FIRST WORDS

THIS message is a struggle to make real to the modern church the hidden wealth of an almost unknown truth of the Word of God.

The writer has felt for years that the disciples had a power to which we are utterly strangers, and that this power should belong to the church.

He has been seeking a solution to this problem and believes that this book will be an unveiling of the hidden spring.

We trust that others will build upon this foundation and that before the return of our Lord, a portion, at least, of the body of believers will be living in the freshness of the power of the early church.

If the book helps you, pass it on.

Chapter I

THE WHY OF THE BOOK

EVERAL years ago I was holding meetings in a city in Tennessee. One afternoon, while giving an address on "The Name of Jesus" a lawyer interrupted me, asking:

"Do you mean to say that Jesus gave us the 'Power of Attorney' the Legal Right to use His Name?"

I said to him, "Brother, you are a lawyer and I am a layman. Tell me—*did* Jesus give us the 'Power of Attorney?'

He said, "If language means anything, then Jesus gave to the church the Power of Attorney."

Then I asked him, "What is the value of this Power of Attorney?"

He answered, "It depends upon how much there is back of it, how much authority, how much power this Name represents."

Then I began the search to find how much power and authority Jesus had.

Then This Book Came

The measure of His ability is the measure of the value of that Name, and all that is invested in that Name belongs to us, for Jesus gave us the unqualified use of His Name.

John 16:24, "Hitherto have ye asked nothing in my name: ask, and ye shall receive that your joy may be made full."

Jesus, here, not only gives us the use of His Name but He also declares that the prayer, prayed in His Name will receive His special attention.

"Whatsoever ye shall ask of the Father in My Name, He will give it to you."

Jesus says, "You ask of the Father in My Name; I will endorse that, and the Father will give it to you."

This puts prayer on a purely legal basis for He has given us the legal right to use His Name.

As we take our privileges, and rights, in the new Covenant and pray in Jesus' Name, it passes out of our hands into the hands of Jesus; He then assumes the responsibility of that prayer, and we know that He said, "Father, I thank Thee that Thou hearest Me, and I know that Thou hearest Me always."

In other words, we know that the Father always hears Jesus, and when we pray in Jesus' Name, it is as though Jesus Himself were doing the praying—He takes our place.

4

Prayer a Business Proposition

This places prayer not only on legal grounds, but makes it a business proposition.

When we pray, we take Jesus' place here to carry out His will, and He takes our place before the Father.

He said that it should not only cover our prayer life but it also can be used in our combat against the unseen forces that surround us.

"And these signs shall accompany them that believe," or literally 'the believing ones'—every child of God is a believing one—"In My Name they shall cast out demons; they shall speak with new tongues; they shall take up serpents; if they drink any deadly thing, it shall in no wise hurt them; they shall lay hands on the sick, and they shall recover."

Here, He is revealing His part in the Great Commission.

In that great document, He says, "All authority has been given unto Me in heaven and on earth.

"I am sending you out to make disciples of all nations.

"Lo, I am with you always."

He is with us in the Power and Authority of His Name.

What does the Name mean to the Father, to the Church, and to Satan?

To the Father, it must mean more than our hearts or minds will ever grasp, but we can suggest a little of the wealth that the Father has stored in that Name. *after resurrection?*

First, He inherited a more excellent Name than any of the angels as the First Begotten Son. *from the dead*

Second, God gave to Him a Name above every name that at the Name of Jesus every knee should bow in the three worlds.

Third, by His conquest over sin, Satan, disease, death, hell, and the grave He acquired a Name that is above all names.

When Jesus gave us the legal right to use this Name, the Father knew all that that Name would imply when breathed in prayer by oppressed souls, and it is His joy to recognize that Name.

So the possibilities enfolded in that Name are beyond our understanding, and when He says to the Church, "Whatsoever ye shall ask of the Father in My Name," He is giving us a signed check on the resources of heaven and asking us to fill it in.

It would pay the Church to begin an exhaustive study of the resources of Jesus in order to get a measurement of the wealth that Name holds for her today.

Chapter II

HOW HE OBTAINED HIS NAME

BEFORE we go further in the study of the Name of Jesus, it would be well for us to know something of the Man, see His standing in heaven, His achievements in the Plan of Redemption and the glory and honor that belongs to Him today as He sits at the Right Hand of the Majesty on High.

Let us turn to Hebrews 1:1-4:

"God having of old time spoken unto the fathers in the prophets by divers portions and in divers manners, (a message here and a message there), hath at the end of these days spoken unto us in His Son, Whom He appointed heir of all things, through Whom also He made the worlds; Who being the effulgence of His glory, and the very image of His substance, and upholding all things by the Word of His power, when He had made purification of sins, sat down on the right hand of the Majesty on High; having become by so much better than the angels, as He hath inherited a more excellent Name than they."

God spoke through men of old by special illumination of their minds but in these last days He speaks unto us in the Person of His Son.

It is more than through Him; it is more than by Him; it is God manifest in the flesh, carrying out His will, speaking His own inner thoughts in the life and acts of the Son.

Not only did He speak through Jesus but more especially was God manifest in the Son—it was God in Christ, and from this new Throne, the Body of His Son, He is speaking to man in a new revelation of Himself.

To this Son Whom He appointed heir of all things and Who being the outshining of His very glory and the very image of His substance and upholding all things by the Word of His power—when He had made a substitution for sins, when He had satisfied every claim of justice and met every need of man, He sat down at the right hand of the Majesty on High—the highest seat in the universe.

When God speaks through man, He must absolutely take possession of the man so the man will not use his reasoning faculties.

But in the case of Jesus, it was not possession—it was the Eternal Son Himself.

He could say, "Father, give Me the glory I had with Thee before the worlds were."

He remembered His place in the Father's bosom.

He could say, "I came out from the Father. I came into the world."

Again, "I leave the world, and go unto the Father."

"Have I been so long time with you and dost Thou not know Me? He that hath seen Me hath seen the Father."

He was the revelation of the Father.

He did not have to imitate God—He was God!

His Three-Fold Greatness

Some men are born to a great name as a czar or a king; others make their name great by achievements or have a great name conferred upon them.

Jesus is great because He inherited a great Name; His Name is great because of achievements; He is great because a great Name was conferred upon Him.

He inherited a greater Name than any angelic being, and as a Son, He is heir of all things, and through Him the ages have been brought into being.

He is the effulgence—the very outshining of the Father.

His Name comes to Him as an Inheritance; and what it must have been to have Inherited this Name from His great Father-God!

In Philippians 2:9, 10 we find: "Wherefore also God highly exalted Him and gave unto Him the Name which is above every Name that at the Name of Jesus every knee should bow of the beings in heaven and the beings on earth, and the beings under the earth, and that every tongue should confess that Jesus Christ is Lord to the glory of God, the Father."

It tells us in Hebrews that He Inherited a greater Name than the angels, here it declares that God gave unto Him the Name which is above every name.

The inference is that there was a Name known in heaven, unknown elsewhere, and this Name was kept to be conferred upon some one who should merit it: and Jesus, as we know Him—the Eternal Son as He is known in the bosom of the Father—was given this Name, and at this Name every knee shall bow in the three worlds—Heaven, Earth, and Hell—and every tongue shall confess that He is Lord of the three worlds to the glory of God, the Father.

This Is the Man

It is this Being Who has given us the right to use His Name.

In Ephesians 1:17 we find a prayer by Paul—a most unusual prayer.

He prays that the Father will open the eyes of our understanding that we may know something of the riches of the Father's inheritance in us, and then, that our eyes may be opened that we may see what is the exceeding greatness of His power on our behalf who believe.

He declares it is according to the working of the strength of God's might which was wrought in the dead body of Jesus when He raised Him from among the dead; and when He raised Him and made Him to sit at His right hand in the heavenlies far above all rule, and authority, and power, and dominion; and every name that is named not only in this age but in that which is to come; and He gave Him to be Head over all things for the benefit of His Church, which is His Body—the fullness of Him that filleth all things in all.

He not only Inherited a more excellent Name than any other being in the universe—God not only Gave Him a Name before which every being in the three worlds shall bow and confess His Lordship—but here, God has Given to Him a Name which is above every name, and He has seated Him in the highest place in the universe, and has made Him Head over all things.

For What Purpose?

God has made this investment for the benefit of the Church; He has made this deposit on which the Church has a right to draw for Her every need.

He has given to Him the Name that has within it the fullness of the Godhead, the wealth of the Eternities, and love of the heart of the Father-God: and, that Name is given us.

We have the right to use that Name against our enemies.

We have the right to use it in our petitions.

We have the right to use it in our praises and worship.

That Name has been given unto us.

But this is only the beginning of the wonders and the value of the greatness of that Name.

In Colossians 2:15 we get a deeper view of His conquest of the Satanic forces just before He rose from the dead: "Having despoiled the principalities and the powers, He made a show of them openly, triumphing over them in it."

The picture here is of Christ in the dark regions of the lost, in awful combat with the hosts of darkness.

It gives us a glimpse of the tremendous battle and victory that Jesus won before He rose from the dead.

The margin reads: "Having put off from Himself, the principalities and powers."

It is evident that the whole demon host, when they saw Jesus in their power simply intended to swamp Him, overwhelm Him and they held Him in fearful bondage until the cry came forth from the throne of God that Jesus had met the demands of justice; that the sin-problem was settled and man's redemption was a fact.

8

The Mighty Victor

When this cry reached the dark regions, Jesus rose and hurled back the hosts of darkness, and met Satan in awful combat as described in Hebrews 2:14:

"In order that through death, He might paralyze him that held the dominion of death—that is, the devil." (Rotherham)

In other words, after Jesus had put off from Himself the demon forces and the awful burden of guilt, sin, and sickness that He carried with Him down there, He grappled with Satan, conquered him, and left him paralyzed, whipped and defeated.

The words that Jesus spoke are fulfilled in Luke 11:21-22: "When a strong man fully armed guardeth his own court, his goods are in peace: but when a stronger man than he shall come upon him, and overcome him, he taketh from him his whole armor wherein he trusted, and divideth his spoils."

So when Christ rose from the dead, He not only had the keys of death and of hell but He had the very armor in which Satan trusted.

He has defeated the devil, He has defeated all hell, and He stands before the three worlds—heaven, earth, and hell—as the undisputed victor over man's ancient destroyer.

He conquered Satan before his own cohorts—his own servants in the dark regions of the damned, and there He stood in that dread place, the absolute victor and Master.

Is it any wonder, that fresh from such tremendous victories, He should say to the disciples, "All authority has been given unto Me in heaven and in earth"?

He stands as the Master and the Ruler of the Universe.

His Name now is above every name, and at His Name we can understand how every knee shall bow and all this authority and power that Jesus gained by His mighty conquest is in that Name—and He has given that Name to us.

The authority that He has won is delegated to us in the use of His Name.

All He was, is in that Name; all He is today, is in that Name—and that Name is ours.

Jesus was given that Name, that He might give it to us.

He gave His Name to us that we might carry out the will of the Father in this dispensation in which we are living.

We know the early Church utilized this authority.

The Early Church acted for Jesus in His stead.

They wrought miracles and the miracles opened doors for ministry and service.

Authority

It gave authority to their credentials—a standing in the communities where they preached.

In the Name of Jesus Christ of Nazareth "Silver + gold have I none, but such as I have I give unto you" Acts 3:6

They had the coin of the unseen Kingdom.

The Omnipotence of God was invested in that Name in the Early Church, and the disciples used it with a fearless abandonment that is absolutely thrilling!

They believed in God! _They believed God!_

They lived and walked in the realm of the supernatural.

former RAIN It was the days of God on earth to the people where they ministered.

The Use of the Name

It might be well for us now to look at the promises Jesus made in regard to the use of His Name.

"And whatsoever ye shall ask in My Name, that will I do that the Father may be glorified in the Son." John 14:13.

magnify extol Praise This is a striking promise when we realize that Jesus is seated at the Right Hand of the Father—that Jesus holds the highest position in the universe as the Head of the Church.

Here is the charter promise: "Hitherto ye have asked nothing in My Name. Ask and ye shall receive that your joy may be made full." John 16:24.

Jesus says, "Hitherto, or up to this time, you have never prayed in My Name, but now, whatsoever ye shall ask of the Father in My Name, He will give it you."

This promise is the most staggering statement that perhaps ever fell from the lips of the Man of Galilee—that we are to have the use of His Name, that Name of Omnipotence.

He does not say, "If we believe," or "if we have faith."

This Name has been given to us. It is ours!

What is mine, I do not need faith to use.

When we are born into the Family of God, the right to use the Name and the privilege to use it comes with the new birth.

All the authority vested in that Name is given to us to bring glory to the Name of the Father—that the Father may be glorified in the Son.

This Son Who was an outcast on the earth and crucified—hung naked before the world—His Name shall go ringing down through the ages.

Wherever the shame of the crucifixion has gone, the glory and might and power and honor of that Name will go.

Wherever men have ridiculed Jesus, that Name will go.

Wherever men have cursed that Man, that Name will go with its Omnipotence, its might and power, shedding blessings and healing and comfort upon the human race, and honor and glory to God, the Father.

He now is to be with us in the power of that Name—that Name is to take His place.

All that He could do locally then can be done locally now by every believer.

10

In other words, He multiplies Himself as rapidly as He multiplies the Church, for the weakest son has a legal right now to all the grace, and might, and power, and blessing, and health, and healing, and life enwrapped in the Person Who bore that Name.

All that Jesus was, His Name is.

All that Jesus was, that Name will ever be during this dispensation.

That Name has lost none of the power of the Man Who bore it.

In these Scriptures, we have seen that the Father has lifted Him to the highest position in the universe.

He has conferred upon Him the highest Name in the universe.

He has bestowed upon Him honor, and glory and power, and seated Him at His own right hand in the heavenlies, far above every known authority; and now, all this honor, this glory, this authority, this power, is vested in the Name of Jesus, and this Name is given to us.

New Land Ahead

Oh, that our eyes were open; that our souls would dare rise into the realm of Omnipotence where the Name would mean to us all that the Father has invested in it, that we would act up to our high privileges in Christ Jesus.

This is practically an unexplored tableland in Christian experience.

Here and there, some of us have experienced the authority vested in the Name of Jesus.

We have seen the lame walk, the deaf hear, the blind see; those on the verge of death brought back instantly to health and vigor; but, so far, none of us have been able to take a permanent place in our privileges and abide where we may enjoy the fullness of this mighty power.

But we have a conviction that before the Lord Jesus returns, there will be a mighty army of believers who will learn the secret of living in the Name, of reigning in life, living the victorious, transcendent, resurrection life of the Son of God among men.

If our minds could only grasp the fact that Satan is paralyzed, stripped of his armor by the Lord Jesus, and that disease and sickness are servants of this Man; that at His voice, they must depart, it would be easy to live in this Resurrection Realm.

You remember in Matt. 8, when the centurion talked with Jesus, he said. "But speak the Word and my servant will be healed, for I myself am a man set under authority, and I say to this one, Go, and he goeth: to another, Come, and he cometh.

11

You have been set over diseases, as I am set over these hundred men, and am called a centurion; so you are Master over disease and sickness, over demons and the laws of nature.

All you have to do is to speak and your servants obey, as I speak and my servants obey."

In this beautiful illustration, we see that the centurion had risen to a higher plane of spiritual appreciation of Jesus than most believers enjoy today.

Chapter III

WHAT IS BACK OF THE NAME

HERE has never been a more intense battle over the Deity of the Man of Galilee than is being waged today.

The great Body of the Church do not see — as they never have seen — the issue squarely; neither have they realized the result of this struggle.

Unfortunately, we have arrayed against the Deity of Christ a body of semi-intellectuals.

There are scarcely a half dozen who belong to the first rank, either of scholastic or intellectual strength, that have been engaged on either side.

The debates that have been staged in different parts of the country have savored more of the barn-storming tactics of the modern political demagogue than of cold-blooded intellectual investigation into the merits of the issue.

The Deity of the Man of Galilee is the crux of Christianity.

If this can be successfully challenged, then Christianity has lost its heart and it will cease to function; it will become a dead religion.

There is no denial that the challenge of His Deity has already begun its reactionary effect upon society.

If Jesus is not Deity, He is not Lord.

If He is not Lord, then He cannot interfere with our moral activities.

If He is not Lord, then the laws that have been founded upon His teachings have lost their force.

The morals that surround marriage with its lofty ideals have no basis of fact.

If Jesus of Nazareth is not a revelation from God with Divine authority, then He is but a man.

If He is but a man, all that we have built around Him must be destroyed, and we have built around this Man our modern civilization.

He has been the inspiration of young men: they have kept themselves clean and pure as they have looked upon His wonder life and sought to win His smile.

Young women in the secret of their chamber have looked upon the face of the Man of Galilee and have pledged to preserve the purity of their womanhood that they might be worthy of the love and confidence of the Man Who died two thousand years ago for humanity.

Children have been incited to obedience and purity by the example and teachings of that Man.

Business men have been deterred from crooked dealings

by the consciousness that one day they would meet that Man and give an account of the deeds done in their office.

Men of all walks of life have felt a strange kinship with this Man Who walked the shores of Galilee, solitary among a multitude.

To say He was but a good man is an insult.

To say that He was the highest expression of Deity in humanity is to throw the lie into His face.

Jesus is or He is not what He said He was.

We have no record of His sayings nor of His doings outside the four Gospels, and if we repudiate them, then we have but a mythical picture of the Man.

If we challenge one of them, we have a right to challenge all of them: either He stands or falls on those four biographical sketches.

If He is not the Son of God, who is He?

I want to believe that He is an Incarnation.

I want to believe that He dealt with the sin problem.

I want to believe that He died for my sins and that He rose again for my justification.

I want to believe that He is seated at God's right hand today as the Intercessor and Mediator of the human race.

I want to believe that what He said about heaven is true: "In my Father's house are many mansions. I go to prepare a place for you, and if I go and prepare a place for you, I will come again and receive you unto myself."

Skepticism holds no guaranty for my future.

Civilization has not only been builded around this Man, but He has been builded into civilization.

If you destroy His character, His standing, His place, then civilization must disintegrate.

The wave of crime and lawlessness that is sweeping over the land is but a by-product of the modernists' challenge of His integrity.

Chapter IV

THE USE OF THE NAME

IT MIGHT be a helpful study for us to notice the Name in the plan of salvation and its relation to the believer in his Christian life.

"And she shall bring forth a Son; and thou shalt call His Name Jesus, for it is He that shall save His people from their sins. Behold, the virgin shall be with child, and shall bring forth a Son, and they shall call His Name Immanuel, which is, being interpreted, God with us." Matt. 1:21, 23.

The Name "Jesus" is inseparably connected with salvation.

The very Name is filled with music to a repentant soul.

"And in none other is there salvation: for neither is there any other name under heaven, that is given among men, wherein we must be saved." Acts 4:12.

It is the one Name through which the sinner approaches the Great Father God; it is the one Name that gives him a hearing; it is the one Name that unveils to him the mediatorial ministry of Jesus.

"Baptizing them into the Name of the Father and of the Son and of the Holy Spirit."

"Repent ye and be baptized every one of you in the Name of Jesus Christ unto the remission of sins and ye shall receive the gift of the Holy Spirit."

Not only are we saved by the Name, but the believer is baptized into the Name.

And we find in the same verse that not only are we baptized into the Name, but on the ground of the Name we shall receive the gift of the Holy Spirit.

Then Jesus gave us these promises of the use of His Name in prayer.

"Whatsoever ye shall ask in My Name, that will I do that the Father may be glorified in the Son. If ye shall ask anything in My Name, that will I do. If ye love Me, ye will keep My commandments." John 14:13-15.

"Hitherto have ye asked nothing in My Name: ask, and ye shall receive, that your joy may be made full." John 16 :24.

In Acts 3:1-6 we hear Peter saying, "Silver and gold have I none, but what I have, that give I thee. In the Name of Jesus Christ of Nazareth, walk."

Men are baptized into the Name; men pray in the Name; now, in that Name the impotent and helpless are made to walk.

In Acts 16 :18 we see the Apostle Paul casting a demon out of a possessed girl, setting her free, and stirring the city of

Ephesus to the very foundation.

What power that Name has for the Church today!

"For where two or three are gathered together in My Name, there am I in the midst of them." Matt. 18:20.

The assemblies were taught that when they met, they gathered about that Name.

What a strange hush must have come upon the hearts of the disciples when they realized as they gathered in their little meetings that that Name was the center around which everything revolved!

That their prayers were addressed through that Name and in that Name the sick were healed; in that Name the demons were cast out: in that Name the Holy Spirit came upon believers; in that Name they worshipped; in that name—the Name of their absent Lord—all the work of the Early Church was wrought.

In Col. 3 :17 they were taught to do all things in that Name.

Eph. 5:20, to give thanks always for all things in that Name.

In 1 Cor. 6:11 they were washed, sanctified, justified in that Name.

Hebrews 13:15, Make confession to His Name.

James 5:14 Anointing the sick in the Name of the Lord.

I John 3:23 "And this is His commandment, that we should believe in the Name of His Son Jesus Christ, and love one another, even as He gave us commandment."

The new commandment was that they love one another and believe in the Name.

We can see by this, that the Name of Jesus touched every phase of the Church life, in those early days; that it filled a place in their thought, in their prayer and in their preaching of which we are utterly ignorant today.

May the Lord open the eyes of our hearts that we may know the riches of the glory of God that are hidden in that Name.

Chapter V

IN MY NAME YE SHALL CAST OUT DEMONS

OST of the readers of this book know what they are worth financially.

If you are a farmer, you know practically every rod of land that your deed covers.

If you own city property, or if you rent, you know every room in the house.

In this grasping world of ours, we attempt to utilize all our possessions; but in the spiritual world, how few of us really know, possess, or enjoy what our deed covers.

The spiritual life is so little understood by even the wisest of us.

You remember that Jesus said as He left the disciples, "In My Name ye shall cast out demons," and you also remember that a large part of His ministry was filled with combats with the unseen hosts of darkness.

One would naturally think in reading our modern religious literature, and listening to the average preacher's sermon, that demons had gone out of existence, or else they had been herded together in the slums of the city and were spending their entire time among the lower strata of humanity.

Years ago I was led to study this subject.

I found that the Scriptures taught a great deal about demons, their habits, influence, and power over men.

When Paul was writing to the Ephesian Church, he told them that their combat was, "Not against flesh and blood, but against the principalities, against the powers, against the world-rulers of this darkness."

Writing to the Colossians, he said: "Epaphras, who is one of you, a servant of Christ Jesus, saluteth you, always striving for you in his prayers, that ye may stand perfect and fully assured in all the will of God."

You notice that the word "striving" literally means to wrestle, struggle, combat.

With whom was he struggling? With whom was this agonizing?

Surely not with the Father: the eternal purpose of the Father is to bless men.

We know that prayer cannot change God's purpose, in any ordinary sense of the word.

Prayer may accelerate God, or stir Him up to come to our rescue, or enlist His cooperation and sympathy and help in a time of need; but all through the Revelation there is breathed out here and there the fact of a hidden force that is intelligently warring against the purpose of God.

In my own ministry for years, I found a great deal of trouble, that perhaps every preacher or evangelist finds, with certain types of people who were always trying and never seemed to get settled in God.

They were always standing up for prayers but never seemed to get any farther.

Another class really seemed to get the light, but were held by some unseen powers.

These people naturally caused me a great deal of trouble— I wondered how I could help them, and one day I was strangely led beyond myself to command that unseen power broken over a person whom it was holding.

I prayed in the Name of Jesus.

I cried: "In the Name of Jesus, I command your power broken over this life."

Instantly, the person was delivered, and I stood amazed at the effect.

A strange fear came over me that I had been able to exercise, by this simple command in Jesus' Name, this marvelous power, and since that time, I have seen many startling results in revival services through using the Name of Jesus.

I found that the reason many men did not accept Jesus as their Saviour was because they were held by the power of demons.

The people are hungry; they want deliverance from sin; they crave eternal life, but they are unable, many of them, to break loose from the bonds that are holding them.

Hundreds of people have said to me, "I cannot become a Christian. I want to, but something holds me."

I have simply laid my hand on their shoulder and said, "In the Name of Jesus of Nazareth, I command the power that holds you, broken. Now, in His mighty Name, get on your feet."

With tears of joy, they have obeyed.

I have prayed with men who were held by habits—tobacco, liquor, lusts, and, in the same mighty Name, I have seen them delivered, usually instantaneously.

I have found Christians who were unable to testify or lead in prayer in public meetings, who felt their mouths closed while their hearts cried for liberty.

I have scarcely met a case, for whom I have prayed in the Name, and over whom I have commanded the power broken, but what they have had immediate deliverance.

In cases of Divine Healing, I have seen some cases that would move the country, had they known of them.

A woman who was almost blind was healed by the power of the Name of Jesus, so that today she can read without glasses.

Some have been cured of heart disease and various other infirmities.

Many of those cases found it very difficult to take their healing.

I prayed for them several times, and found that the difficulty lay in the fact that they were held, that they were bound by the power of demons. They were delivered when I said, "In the Name of Jesus, demons leave this body."

I cannot conceive how successful work can be done today, or how believers can be in a place of continual victory, unless they know that the source of their danger lies in demoniacal power, and that the power to conquer it is in the Name of Jesus of Nazareth, the Son of God.

The more quickly we recognize that the very air about us is filled with hostile forces, who are attempting to destroy our fellowship with the Father, and to deprive us of our usefulness in the service of our Master, the better it will be for us.

Three things are necessary in order to pray and take deliverance and victory over demons.

First, we must be children of God.

Second, we must not have any unconfessed or unforgiven sin in the heart, for if we do, the demons will laugh at our prayers.

Third, we must know the power of the Name of Jesus, and know how to use it.

Read the Book of Acts carefully, and notice how the disciples used the Name.

Readers, if your own life has been defeated and hemmed in by the power of the Adversary, rise up in that Almighty Name of Jesus; hurl back the Enemy; take your deliverance; go, and set others free.

In His Name

What does the expression "in His Name" mean?

We know that the expression "in Christ" as used about one hundred and thirty times in the New Testament, shows us the believer's position, his Legal Standing, his place in the family and in the purposes or program of God.

When Jesus gave to the Early Church the Right to use His Name, that Right meant that they were to represent Him; they were acting in His stead, and when they prayed in Jesus' Name, it was as though Jesus Himself were praying.

I mean that we are taking Christ's place and acting as Christ's representatives.

Christ is at the Right Hand of the Father—we are here as His representatives, not only collectively, but individually.

19

When we pray in Jesus' Name, we are taking the place of the absent Christ; we are using His Name, using His authority, to carry out His will on the earth.

When we say, "Father, we ask this in Jesus' Name," we are praying representatively.

We are saying, "Father, Jesus is up there at Thy Right Hand and He gave us the Power of Attorney to carry out your will on earth. So here is this great need. We ask Thee in His Name to meet it."

That need may be for finances, it may be for power in ministry; it may be for salvation of souls; it may be for the healing of a sick one—but we take Jesus' place and use Jesus' Name just as though Jesus Himself were here.

The only difference is that instead of Jesus doing it, we are doing it for Him; we are doing it at His command.

He has given to us the same authority He had when He was here, and the believer's position in Christ gives him the same Standing with the Father that Christ had when He was here.

This unlimited use of the Name of Jesus reveals to us the implicit confidence that the Father has in the Church.

This in itself is a challenge.

The simplicity of Peter's use of the Name of Jesus in the Book of Acts compels us to believe that Peter knew he was acting in Jesus' stead, with the same authority that Jesus had.

You will notice he does not stop even to pray for a sick one: all he does is to say, "In Jesus' Name, rise and walk."

There is no hint that he attempted to exercise what we call "faith" in any manner; it reduced itself to a simple business proposition with the Early Church—they remembered what the Master said and what He said, was true, to them.

He said, "Whatsoever ye shall ask the Father in My Name, I will give it you."

They did not argue about it; they did not worry about it; they did not stop to analyze what it meant—all they did was to act on the Words of Jesus.

They did not understand all that Paul afterwards revealed to us in Romans, Galatians, and Ephesians, but they did know that Jesus had given them a Right to use that Name and they entered into that Right with the simplicity of a child.

It seems to me that this is what we need to do today.

"In My Name ye shall cast out demons; in My Name ye shall lay hands on the sick and they shall recover."

This was given to believers, and we are believers.

"Whatsoever ye shall ask the Father in My Name, He will give it you," is a declaration that is simple enough for anyone to understand.

20

We have been baptized into that Name publicly; and spiritually, we have been put into Christ by the New Birth so that we now are in the Vine as one of the branches, and the Vine is Christ.

We are in Christ, and being in Christ, we have a right to use His Name, and so in that Name we act representatively, legally.

This glorifies the Father; this magnifies Jesus; this answers the need of humanity.

Here is supernatural power that is available to every believer.

It is not a question of education or ordination but merely a question of my apprehending my own true position in Christ, and there using the power that has been legally given to me and to every believer.

Oh, the wonder and grace of God!

at His command

(1) He told us to use HIS NAME
AND
(2) TO CAST OUT DEMONS; Heal the sick; RAISE THE DEAD

Chapter VI

MAN AND MIRACLES

JESUS! The very Name has within it miracle working power, even to this day, though nearly two thousand years have rolled away since He walked with men.

Jesus, the Galilean, was a miracle worker.

Jesus' life was a miracle.

His wisdom and teachings were miraculous.

He lived and walked in the realm of the miraculous.

He made miracles common.

His death was a miracle.

His resurrection was a miracle.

His appearances were miraculous.

His ascension was a staggering miracle.

But perhaps the most outstanding miracle of all those wonder days was the event of Pentecost.

From the upper room, went forth men and women boldly to testify of Jesus' Name, who fifty days before shrank in fear from the very names of the High Priest and his associates.

Peter, the trembling, fearful Peter, is now clothed with a power and fearlessness that is inexplicable; he goes out and faces the Sanhedrin, Senate, and High Priesthood with a courage that amazes us.

A stream of miracles flowed from the hands of the apostles that upset Judaism and shook the Roman government to its foundation.

They made a discovery—the Name of the Man Whom they had loved, Whom they had seen nailed to that cross in nakedness, now has power equal to the power that He, Himself exercised when He was among them.

The sick were healed, the dead were raised, demons were cast out by simply breathing that Name over the afflicted ones.

What a stream of miraculous love, life, hope, and joy showered from the ministry of those humble Galileans.

Those first thirty-three years of early history as seen in Acts, were sample years of the acts of the Church until the return of Her Lord and Master.

Man is the offspring of the miracle worker.

The miracle working desire is embedded deep in the consciousness of man.

Christianity is based on a series of miracles culminating in Pentecost.

Miracles Normal

Christianity began in miracles; it is propagated by miracles.

Every new birth is a miracle; every answer to prayer is a miracle, every victory over temptation is a miracle.

When Reason takes the place of the miraculous, Christianity loses its virility, fascination, and fruitfulness.

Christianity is not a religion.

Christianity is the life of God in man.

Christianity was the unveiling of the heart and nature of the Great Father-God in the Man Jesus.

There could not be a religion that would appeal to humanity that was not founded upon miracles and propagated by miracles.

Man craves a miracle working God today.

Whenever there arises a man or woman whose prayers are heard and answered, the multitudes flock to them.

Man wants a living God.

Man craves a miracle.

The deep seated hunger in the human heart for God is the reason for all religions.

Men are easily deceived by psuedo miracle workers because of this hunger after the supernatural.

One of America's greatest psychologists, who ridiculed the miraculous for over thirty years in his class room at one of the leading universities, finally sat at the feet of the high priestess of Spiritualism and confessed over his own signature in a popular magazine that at last he had found faith in the supernatural.

What a pitiable picture! Turning from the miracle working Jesus to the miracle working Satan.

God created man in His own image and in His own likeness, and through Jesus Christ allows him to become a partaker of His own nature.

This lifts man into the realm of God, and in that realm the Father-God can unveil Himself to His child.

The answer to the universal craving of man for the supernatural is found in the new birth, and indwelling presence of the Holy Spirit, and the Name of Jesus.

Prayer becomes a miracle working force in the world.

Christianity is a Miracle

God is a miracle worker.

Jesus Christ was a miracle, and is a miracle.

The Bible is a miracle Book.

If we take the supernatural out of Christianity, we have a religion.

Miracles are not out of harmony with the desire of humanity.

A miracle worker, either real or false, will draw a greater

congregation than the greatest philosopher or statesman in the world.

This love of the miraculous is not a mark of ignorance but rather an outreaching after the unseen God.

Education does not eliminate the desire for the miraculous in man.

That desire is intensified, as education unveils man's impotence in the presence of the laws of nature and shows him his utter dependence upon the unseen.

It is not a mark of great scholarship, piety, or mental acumen to deny the miraculous.

The Universal Man Believes in Miracles

The Bible is a record of miracles and Divine interventions.

It is history of the outbreakings of the supernatural realm into the natural.

Beginning with Abraham all of the major characters of Old Testament history were miracle workers — or better, God wrought miracles through them.

The thing that lifted Joseph from the prison to the office of premier of Egypt was a miracle.

Israel's deliverance from Egypt's bondage was by a series of miracles that shook Egypt to its very foundation.

The crossing of the Red Sea and the forty years in the wilderness were a series of miracles unparalleled in human history.

The object of these miracles was to separate Israel from the dead gods of Egypt and bind them to the worship of the Living God of Abraham.

Judaism was Judaism as long as the miracle working God was manifest.

When miracles ended, Israel lapsed into heathenism, and only came back into fellowship with their God after a series of staggering miracles.

Had we space, it would be interesting to study the miracles of the Conquest of Canaan, the period of the Kings, of the Four Great Miracles recorded in Daniel that sent Israel back from captivity into their own land, free from idolatry, establishing a precedent of a nation of slaves set free, and sent to their own country with permission — aye, more — with funds to rebuild their city, their temple, and establish its worship; it has no parallel in human history — it is a distinct and definite miracle.

When Jesus began His public ministry, it was a ministry of miracles.

When the Church began her ministry it was a ministry of miracles.

Every revival since Pentecost that has honored the humble Galilean has been a revival of miracles.

The Church has never been rescued from Her backslidings by great philosophical teachers but humble laymen who have had a new vision of the Christ, of "Him Who is the same yesterday, today, and forever."

We crave the manifest presence of the Spirit in our religious services—a dry, dead meeting has no drawing power but a service where men are being richly blessed in the unfolding of Scripture or the saving of souls, the healing of the sick, or the filling with the Spirit, has a drawing power.

An outpouring of the Spirit is a challenge to a community any time.

All normal men crave the supernatural—they long to see the manifestation of the power of God and to feel the thrill of the touch of the unseen.

Man Demands Miracles

Man was created by a miracle working God—that miracle element is in man.

Man yearns to perform miracles and live in the atmosphere of the supernatural.

This miracle element in man has made him an inventor, discoverer, and investigator.

It has caused him to experiment until he has conquered chemicals, electricity and the air.

It is this element that has given to us the aeroplane, submarine, radio, and wireless, and all the other devices, inventions, and discoveries that make up our modern civilization.

The miracle realm is man's natural realm—he is by creation the companion of the miracle working Father-God.

Sin dethroned man from the miracle realm but through grace he is coming into his own.

It has been a hard struggle for us to grasp the principles of this strange life of faith.

Sin has made us workers—grace would make us trusters.

In the beginning, man's spirit was the dominant force in the world; when he sinned, his mind became dominant—sin dethroned the spirit and crowned the intellect; but grace is restoring the spirit to its place of dominion, and when man comes to recognize the dominance of the spirit, he will live in the realm of the supernatural without effort.

No longer will faith be a struggle and fight but an unconscious living in the realm of God.

The spiritual realm is man's normal home; it places him where communion with God is a normal experience, where faith in the miraculous, miracle-working God is unconscious, where he will exercise the highest type of faith and yet be as unconscious of having exercised faith as he is when he writes a check.

Chapter VII

THE PLACE OF FAITH IN THE USE OF THE NAME

HE prayerful student of the Word is confronted with this fact—that nowhere does Jesus mention Faith or Belief when He is talking about using His Name except in the Future Tense.

Take Mark 16:17, 18 as an illustration:

"And these signs shall accompany them that believe: in My Name they shall cast out demons; they shall speak with new tongues; they shall take up serpents, and if they drink any deadly thing it shall in no wise hurt them; they shall lay hands on the sick and they shall recover."

A literal rendering of that is "the believing ones" shall in My Name do these things.

It is taken for granted that only believers have a Right to the use of the Name of Jesus—the Right to use His Name is a conferred blessing to the Church:—it is a Right that belongs to every child of God.

We have a four-fold right to use the Name.

First, we are born into the family of God and the Name belongs to the family.

Second, we are baptized into the Name and being baptized into the Name, we are baptized into Christ Himself.

Third, it was conferred upon us by Jesus Who gave us the Power of Attorney.

Fourth, we are commissioned as Ambassadors to go and herald this Name among the nations.

Then if this authority is conferred upon us we act as representatives for Christ.

We do this first, on the ground of our birthright, second, on the ground of having been baptized into this Name, and third, that the legal right to use this Name has been conferred upon us.

Last, on the ground that we have been sent out as ambassadors to herald this Name among the nations.

I cannot see where we need to have any special Faith to use the Name of Jesus, because it is legally ours.

If I had a thousand dollars in the bank, it would not require any conscious act of Faith on my part to write a check for one hundred, but if I wanted to draw eleven hundred dollars where I only had one thousand on deposit, that might require Faith.

Some of us have had the unhappy experience of having overdrawn our bank account on earth, but the Finished Work of Jesus Christ has made a deposit for us in the Bank up there that cannot be overdrawn.

It is ours—blessedly, eternally ours. Thank God!

If you are a child, then you are an heir of God—a joint heir with Christ—you have a Right to the use of the Name of Jesus, and if you have this Right, it is because of your place in the family.

I believe the hour will come when large companies of believers will live this simple life of Faith; live it unconsciously, live it daily—they will live in this upper realm where they will see in the Name of Jesus the fullness of the authority and power that was in Christ when He walked on the earth.

We are now in the babyhood stage: we are trying to have faith; we are trying to believe; and we meet together in our services, each one urging the other to do, what he does not do himself.

It would seem in many cases that we are practicing a game of bluff.

Are we using Scriptural expressions and high sounding phrases that have no meaning to our inner consciousness?

Thank God, there are some who are coming to see this new light, which will only come by intensive study and actually thinking through on this problem.

Too many of us are listening to preachers, always listening and never digesting or doing any original thinking—we are what Jesus called "hearers of the Word and not doers."

The instant a man or woman thinks through on this problem, that moment he rises into a new realm of Life in Christ—he actually begins to reign in the realm of Life.

Then he is able to meet demons and diseases on their own plane, and conquer them; able to enjoy the fruits of the Finished Work of Christ and enter into the riches of His inheritance.

Jesus Is In That Name

He is that Name.

All He was, all He did, all He is and all that He ever will be is in that Name now.

He wrought the healing for us; He is healing for us now.

He satisfied the claims of justice and became our righteousness—He is now our righteousness.

He passed down through death and up into life, and He is our Life now.

He gave us life—He is that Life He gave.

He is healing, He is health, He is victory, He is our all and in all.

That Name Is Healing

And when He gave us the right to use His Name to heal the sick, it was simply that we might bring on the scene by the use of that Name the fullness of His finished work, and that

27

the afflicted one might know that in the use of that Name the Living, Healing Christ was present.

It is not trying to believe; it is not trying to take healing.

Believing becomes unnecessary in the modern sense of that term.

That healing is ours; that Name makes it available to us.

That Name is ours, and in that Name is all help, all victory, all power, all health.

Do not try; do not struggle—just use it.

Use that Name with the same freedom that you use your check book.

The money is on deposit; you write the check without exercising any special faith; that is, you are not conscious of exercising it—you do though.

And in the use of Jesus' Name, you do exercise Faith—it is the unconscious faith, the faith that is borne in upon us by evidences that convince us beyond the shadow of a doubt.

Any other kind of faith is abnormal.

At the Second Coming of Christ, it will not require any act of faith to receive immortality—we shall simply be made immortal—we shall be translated.

That is in the plan, in the eternal program of God.

It will not require any special faith to be resurrected—the resurrection is in the program.

His Program

Now, if we understand His program for today, the sick would simply be healed the moment that sickness touched them.

"If the Spirit that raised up Christ Jesus from the dead dwelleth in you, He that raised up Christ Jesus from the dead shall also quicken, (or heal), your mortal bodies by His Spirit that dwelleth in you."

This does not have reference to our Resurrection; it refers to our bodies now (mortal means death—doomed). Our bodies will not be mortal in the grave, neither will the spirit be in them then.

This is a part of the program—the Spirit dwells in us for that purpose.

That is not the only purpose, but that is one of the reasons of His indwelling—to heal our physical bodies of the diseases that are continually attaching themselves to us.

When we understand this, we shall not be trying to exercise faith for our healing, or for any other need—we shall simply recognize the fact that this healing, this need, is in the program, is a part of it, and we shall accept what belongs to us.

Take this Scripture as an illustration:

"Who His own self bare our sins in His body upon the tree that we having died unto sin might live unto righteousness. By whose stripes ye were healed," or by whose bruisings we are healed.

He bore our sins in His body on the tree and He died because of those sins, and we believe that we died with Him— then we do not have to die again to sin.

We Are Alive

He was made alive, and we were made alive with Him.

We died to our sins, we died to our old nature, we died to our diseases, and we rose in the fullness of His life, free from our old sin nature, free from our sins that we had committed, and free from our diseases.

As we come to understand this, we know that our old sin nature hasn't any right, any privilege, to reign over us because it is dead, and we will not accept any imitation of it that Satan may in our ignorance impose upon us, neither will we recognize any condemnation that might come to us through any sins we may have committed in the past, for Christ bore them, and we need never bear them again, neither do we need to suffer any condemnation for them because He was condemned for them, and He bore them.

Consequently, we are free, and there is, "therefore, now, no condemnation to us because we are in Christ Jesus."

The same thing is true with our sicknesses. Isa. 53:4 "He bore our sicknesses and carried our pains." (correct translation)

He was made sick for us and bore our sicknesses; when He rose, the sickness had been put away and He rose in resurrection life; free from the dominion of sickness.

Now, sickness hasn't any right to impose itself upon us and Satan hasn't any right to impose any diseases upon us.

We are free!

And when these diseases and sicknesses come, all we need to do is treat them exactly the same as we treat our old sins.

The devil may try to put us under condemnation by reminding us of our past sins, but we say, "Satan, there is, therefore, now no condemnation upon us, for we are in Christ Jesus. He has dealt with those sins and put them away, and you cannot get them. You may bring back a photograph of them but you cannot get the actual real sin because it has been put away."

My Legal Rights

When he imposes diseases upon me, I have a right to say to him, "Satan, those diseases were borne in the body of Jesus and you have no right to bring their photograph around here, and frighten me with them.

29

"Those diseases were unconditionally put away, and I am free from disease as the body of Jesus was when He rose from the dead. For I am in Christ Jesus and you cannot put those things on me."

And if Satan should attack my body, all I have to do is to call my Father's attention to the fact, and the disease must go, because I am free!

I know that "by His stripes I am healed."

If I am healed, I am healed!

I know that by His resurrection I am justified, and I do not need to be re-justified: I am justified!

I know that by His life I am made alive, and I am alive!

I know that I died with Him; I know that I rose with Him; and I know that I am in Him.

I know that by His stripes I am healed; then I am healed, and if I am healed, I am well—thank God!

I have no more to do with my healing than I have to do with my resurrection, for He is my resurrection! He is my healing!

He said, "I am the resurrection and the life."

He is my resurrection; He is my life; He is my healing; He is my health; He is my victory; He is my all and in all.

Now, I simply recognize the fact that He healed me in His substitutionary work, and because of that I am healed.

The hour is coming when this kind of knowledge will be so common that men and women who are in Christ and walking in Him will be healed the moment they are afflicted, and they will live in perfect health—in body as well as soul and spirit.

They will live like this until their bodies are worn out and they fall asleep in Christ.

There is no more need of our bearing about in our bodies our sicknesses than there is of bearing about in our spiritual nature an unforgiven sin.

His Word True

For the very moment I confess my sins, "He is faithful and righteous to forgive me," and when He forgives me, I am forgiven.

On the same ground, the moment I confess that Satan has put a disease or infirmity upon me, just that moment He is faithful and righteous to heal me, and I am healed!

He healed me of my sin; He now heals me of my sickness—they both come from the same source.

It requires no struggle, no long drawn out siege of struggling after faith and trying to believe.

There is the written Word, and the Eternal Throne of God is back of it.

That Word cannot fail any more than God can fail, and when I confess my sins, I am forgiven.

If I refuse this, if I challenge it, I declare by that challenge or that refusal, that God is a liar, that His Word is not true; that all He has said in the Scripture is a lie.

For all unbelief is a challenge of the integrity of God.

Then this new kind of faith in Him becomes the stabilizer of one's whole spiritual nature.

It is a faith that grows out of the knowledge of God's faithfulness,—of evidences given in the Word, of facts that have become a part of spiritual knowledge so that when the believer is "exercising faith" he unconsciously acts as he does when writing a check for money he knows is in the bank.

Then the greatest need of the hour is not more faith but more knowledge that will produce an unconscious faith in our great, loving Father-God.

The Place Confession Holds

The Church has never given this vital subject a place in its teaching and yet, answered prayer, the use of Jesus' name and Faith are utterly dependent upon it.

"Wherefore, holy brethren, partakers of a heavenly calling, consider the Apostle and High Priest of our confession." (Heb. 3:1)

Christianity is called our confession and in Heb. 4:14, He tells us to "hold fast our confession."

The old version reads "profession," but the Greek means witnessing a confession of our lips.

You understand Romans 10:9-10, "Because if thou shalt confess with thy mouth Jesus as Lord, and shall believe in thy heart that God raised him from the dead, thou shalt be saved: for with the heart man believeth unto righteousness; and with the mouth confession is made unto salvation."

You see the place that confession holds in salvation.

It holds the same place in our Faith walk.

Christianity is a Confession. It is our open confession of what we are in Christ, of what Christ is to us.

Our Faith is gauged by our confession.

We never believe beyond our confession.

It is not a confession of sin; it is the confession of our place in Christ, of our Legal Rights, of what the Father has done for us in Christ and what the Spirit has done in us through the Word and what He is able to do through us.

There is a grave danger of our having two confessions.

One would be the integrity of the Word and the other would be of our doubts and fears.

31

Every time we confess weakness and failure and doubt and fear, we go to the level of them.

We may pray very ardently and very earnestly and declare in our prayers our faith in the Word and yet, the next moment we question whether He heard us or not, for we confess we have not the things for which we prayed.

Our last confession destroys our prayer.

One asked me to pray for his healing. I prayed for him and then he said, "I want you to keep on praying for me." I asked them what he wished me to pray for. He said, "Oh, for my healing." I said, "Prayer will be of no value. You have just denied the Word of God."

The Word says, "That they that believe shall lay hands on the sick and they shall recover, and whatsoever ye shall ask in my name, that will I do."

I prayed the prayer of Faith and he denied it. By his confession, he annulled my prayer and destroyed the effect of my faith.

Your confession must absolutely agree with the Word, and if you have prayed in Jesus' Name, you are to hold fast your confession. It is easy to destroy the effect of your prayer by a negative confession.

Chapter VIII

THE NAME IN THE GOSPELS

"AND she shall bring forth a Son, and thou shalt call His Name Jesus for it is He that shall save His people from their sins." Matt. 1:21.

Little did Mary know the meaning of that angelic visit nor of the command that His Name shall be called Jesus.

That Name has grown until today it fills the whole earth.

That Name means justice, love, righteousness, civilization, invention, discovery, art, literature, music, health, happiness, home; and, yet, in our study we have discovered that that Name means even more.

"Behold, the virgin shall be with child and shall bring forth a Son, and they shall call His Name Immanuel (or Incarnation)." Isa. 7:14.

Immanuel means "God with us" and God with us means the Incarnate One.

"For the Word was made flesh and dwelt among us," and it is the Name of this Incarnate One that is engaging our attention now.

"And ye shall be hated of all men for My Name's sake." Matt. 10:22.

Jesus knew the place His Name would hold among men.

Men would love it enough to die for it; others would hate it enough to commit murder on account of it—this Name that makes sinners tremble and saints rejoice.

"And in His Name shall the Gentiles hope." Matt. 12:21.

How true that is! The Name of Jesus has been the only Name that would stop wars between nations.

That Name bears within it love, life, light, liberty, joy.

"And whoso shall receive one such little child in My Name receiveth Me." Matt. 18:5.

For the first time in human history, little children have a friend—little children can be received in His Name.

And what a judgment He pronounces upon anyone who injures or hurts one of the little ones who have believed in Him or in His Name!

It is peculiarly precious the way Jesus links His Name with the childhood of humanity.

The 20th verse carries us into the mystery of Christ's oneness with believers when they meet together.

"For where two or three are gathered together in My Name, there am I in the midst of them."

"For many shall come in My Name, saying, I am the Christ: and shall lead many astray." Matt 24 :5.

How well Jesus understood what His Name would mean to the world!

He knew that false teachers and imposters would come in His Name and He warns the Church of the danger that shall confront Her down through the ages.

"Go ye, therefore, and make disciples of all the nations, baptizing them into the Name of the Father and of the Son and of the Holy Spirit." Matt. 28:19.

This is the Great Commission and the apostolic formula of baptism.

The Name In the Gospel of Mark

In the Gospel of Mark, there are but four references.

"John said unto Him, Teacher, we saw one casting out demons in Thy Name; and we forbade him, because he followed not us. But Jesus said, Forbid him not; for there is no man who shall do a mighty work in My Name, and be able quickly to speak evil of Me." Mark 9:38-39.

You see that the Name of Jesus was great even before He died; that men were casting out demons and healing the sick in His Name before His death, resurrection, and ascension to the right hand of the Father.

This in itself is a very striking fact and worthy of much meditation.

"And ye shall be hated of all men for My Name's sake, but he that endureth to the end, the same shall be saved." Mark 13:13

Jesus knew the hatred that His Name would engender for His followers in the world and He prepares them by this warning.

"And these signs shall accompany them that believe: in My Name shall they cast out demons; they shall speak with new tongues; they shall take up serpents, and if they drink any deadly thing, it shall in no wise hurt them; they shall lay hands on the sick, and they shall recover." Mark 16:17-18.

This is the Great Commission which He gave to the disciples.

In this Scripture Jesus specifies some of the things that Name will do.

It almost bewilders us when we think that the God of the universe will give to humanity the right to use His Name—will give to men a legal right to use the power and the authority of the Son of God.

That in that Name a mother can lay her hands upon her baby when he is sick and take healing for him.

The Greek here means "the believing ones" shall lay hands on the sick in that Name and they shall recover.

34

That includes every child of God: no special gift, no special faith—just "the believing ones."

Jesus said, "Lo, I am with you always unto the end of the age," and this is His method of being present today.

He has given them the use of His Name, and in the heathen nations where they go as heralds of His grace, they shall do as Paul did on the Island of Melita and many other fields.

In that Name they are to cast out demons; they are to heal the sick and perform other mighty miracles that will arrest the attention of the people and cause them to ask, "Who is this Jesus in Whose Name you work today?"

God never intended there should ever be any change in the methods or ministry down through the ages; only as nations developed, should these methods be broadened, but the miraculous element enfolded in the Name of Jesus should be the means of opening closed doors to the Church everywhere; the sick should be healed; the power of Satan broken over men's lives and captives set free.

All this is to be done in the Name of this Unseen Saviour.

The Name in the Gospel of Luke

The Gospel of Luke has seven references; let us briefly scan them.

"Whosoever shall receive this little child in My Name receiveth Me: and whosoever shall receive Me receiveth Him that sent Me: for he that is least among you all, the same is great." Luke 9:48.

We have the same thought brought out in Matthew.

It is Jesus honoring the little child and giving to the little child its place in the assembly.

It is not enough that our children are taken into the Sunday School but the child has its place in the Church and should receive instructions, not from an unsaved Sunday School teacher, but from a real man or woman of God.

Another striking suggestion is in this verse—"Whosoever shall receive this little child in My Name receiveth Me."

His Name then is equivalent to Himself.

"Inasmuch as ye do it unto one of the least of these, my brethren, ye do it unto Me."

Jesus teaches us the sacredness of His Name.

"John answered and said, Master, we saw one casting out demons in Thy Name: and we forbade him, because he followeth not with us. But Jesus said unto him, Forbid him not: for he that is not against you is for you." Luke 9:49-50.

Jesus said to John, "Forbid him not. Let him go on." Thank God for anyone who is being helped or blessed, whether they walk with us or not.

"And the seventy returned with joy, saying, Lord, even the demons are subject unto us in Thy Name." Luke 10:17.

The disciples had an opportunity of seeing the power of Jesus' Name before the Day of Pentecost.

"Take heed that ye be not led astray: for many shall come in My Name, saying, I am he: and, The time is at hand: go ye not after them." Luke 21:8.

Jesus knew that false prophets would arise and impersonate Him.

In the 12th verse of the same chapter, He said the disciples would be brought up before kings and governors for His Name's sake.

"And that repentance and remission of sins should be preached in His Name unto all the Nations, beginning from Jerusalem." Luke 24:47.

This is a part of the Great Commission that repentance and remission of sins are to be preached in His Name.

How few of the evangelists and preachers have caught a glimpse of this mighty truth—the place of the Name of Jesus in evangelism!

In the 8th chapter of Acts we read that when they listened to Philip preaching the kingdom of God and the Name of Jesus, they were led to accept Christ.

What a small place the Name of Jesus has in the modern Church!

The Name in the Gospel of John

"But as many as received Him, to them gave He the right to become children of God, even to them that believe on His Name." John 1:12.

Salvation here then comes by believing on the Name.

"Now when He was in Jerusalem at the passover, during the feast, many believed on His Name, beholding His signs which He did." John 2:23.

Christianity would have a new element in it if we taught the people intelligently what it meant to believe ON the Name as a sinner and then to believe IN the Name as a believer.

As a sinner, I believe ON the Name; as a believer, I am baptized INTO it, and then I walk and live IN the Name; and this Man is the Head of the Church.

Jesus is the Head: we are the Body.

We are baptized into the Head.

To the Head belongs the Name, and the Head gives us, the Body, the right to live, to walk, to use the power of that Name.

"He that believeth on Him is not judged: he that believeth not hath been judged already, because he hath not believed on the Name of the only begotten Son of God." John 3:18.

Judgment is coming to man because he has not believed on the Name.

"Whatsoever ye shall ask in My Name, that will I do, that the Father may be glorified in the Son. If ye shall ask anything in My Name, that will I do." John 14:13-14.

This is the first time that man had ever been taught to pray in the Name of a Mediator.

Here, Jesus gives to His disciples the unique privilege of praying in His Name.

Up to that time, they had prayer through the High Priest; now, they were to pray through this new High Priest.

Wherever they go, whatever they do, they are to bear with them the Name of this One Who is seated at the right hand of the Father; and Jesus says that the Father is glorified in the Son by our praying and asking in His Name.

"If ye shall ask anything in My Name, that will I do."

Jesus is seated there at the Father's right hand to endorse our petitions when they come up to the Father in His Name.

"That whatsoever ye shall ask of the Father in My Name, He may give it you." John 15:16.

"And in that day ye shall ask Me nothing. Verily, verily, I say unto you, If ye shall ask anything of the Father, He will give it you in My Name. Hitherto have ye asked nothing in My Name: ask, and ye shall receive, that your joy may be made full." John 16:23-24.

This is the Great Charter Promise in the Name of Christ.

In this we can plainly see the legal foundation for a wonderful prayer life for the Church—a legal right to use the Name of Jesus without any restrictions.

If we are children of God, all that is in that Name belongs to us.

It is not a question of our worthiness: it is a question of His standing in heaven, and as sons and daughters we take our place and claim our rights.

Chapter IX

THE BOOK OF ACTS

CTS 2:38, "Repent and be baptized every one of you, in the Name of Jesus Christ."

This first use of the Name of Jesus must have struck the Jews with a peculiar force.

Fifty days before, they had hung Him stark naked upon a cross; now, three thousand of them cry out, "Men and brethren, what shall we do?"

Peter answers, "Repent ye and be baptized every one of you in the Name of Jesus Christ unto the remission of your sins."

This meant a break with Judaism, although it was not clearly in their minds yet, but to be baptized into that Name was to put on that Name and bear the stigma of that Name among their fellows.

The First Miracle in the Name

In the 3rd chapter, we get its first public use.

Peter and John are going up to the Temple to worship, (they had not yet been separated from the temple worship), and as they arrived at the door of the temple which is called "Beautiful," they saw a cripple lying in his dirt and helplessness, with outstretched hands beseeching an offering.

Peter and John, fastening their eyes on him, said, "Look on us."

And he, expecting to receive something, looked up.

Then said Peter, "Silver and gold have I none but what I have, that give I thee."

I can see the disappointed look followed by a mystified expression in his eyes as he looked upon those two humble fishermen.

Peter continued, "In the Name of Jesus Christ of Nazareth, walk!"

And immediately a thrill passed through his body; Peter reached down, grasped him by the hand and lifted him to his feet; and those ankles that had been useless from babyhood were filled with the strength of manhood.

For the first time in his life this man could leap, run, and walk.

During all of his babyhood days he had watched others playing while he himself was unable to take any part in their sport, but now this impotent, useless member of society throbbed with health and life.

He rushed into the temple, leaping, jumping, and shouting praises to God; finally, he turned and grasped Peter and John by the hands while the multitude gathered about them, and Peter declared, "Why fasten ye your eyes upon us, as though by our own power we made this man to walk. The God of Abraham, Isaac, and Jacob—the God of our fathers hath glorified this Man Jesus Whom ye delivered up and denied in the face of Pilate when he determined to release him. But ye denied the Holy One and asked for a murderer to be granted unto you. Ye killed the Author of Life Whom God raised from the dead, whereof we are witnesses. And on the ground of faith in His Name hath His Name made this man strong whom ye behold and know."

How the Early Church Used the Name

This is the first recorded miracle in the Name of Jesus.

Note how the Scripture reads:

"On the ground of faith in His Name hath His Name made this man strong, whom ye behold and know. Yea, the faith which is through Him hath given Him this perfect soundness in the presence of you all." Acts 3:16.

For the first time, we come in vital contact with this strange power vested in the Name of Jesus.

This miracle created a sensation; the disciples were arrested, put in jail until the morrow.

Through this miracle the number of disciples had increased to about five thousand.

"And it came to pass on the morrow, that their rulers and elders and scribes were gathered together in Jerusalem; and Annas the high priest was there, and Caiaphas, and John, and Alexander, as were the kindred of the high priest. And when they had set them in the midst, they inquired, "By what power, or in what name, have ye done this?" Then Peter, filled with the Holy Spirit, said unto them, "Ye rulers of the people, and elders, if we this day are examined concerning a good deed done to an impotent man, by what means this man is made whole; be it known unto you all, and to all the people of Israel, that in the Name of Jesus Christ of Nazareth, Whom ye crucified, Whom God raised from the dead, even in Him doth this man stand here before you whole. He is the stone which was set at nought of you the builders, which was made the head of the corner. And in none other is there salvation: for neither is there any other Name under heaven, that is given among men, wherein we must be saved." Acts 4:5-12.

Consternation in the Sanhedrin

They wanted to know what power or what means they used, or by what name they had done that mighty act.

Peter told them it was in the Name of Jesus of Nazareth,

Whom they crucified, Whom God had raised from the dead—that in His Name did this man stand before them whole.

Then the Council acted.

They said, "What shall we do to these men; For that indeed a notable miracle hath been wrought through them, is manifest to all that dwell in Jerusalem; and we cannot deny it." Acts 4:16.

No matter how much we may wish to deny it, the fact stands before us: a man who had been impotent for years was suddenly healed in the Name of Jesus.

No miracle like this had ever happened before in human history; it shook the Sanhedrin to the foundation—their wisest men were in confusion; the disciples were ordered aside for a moment while the Sanhedrin conferred, and in their fear they threatened:

"But that it spread no further among the people, let us threaten them, that they speak henceforth to no man in this Name. And they called them, and charged them not to speak nor teach at all in the Name of Jesus." Acts 4:17-18.

It does not seem that they objected so much to the teaching of His resurrection but they feared the power of that Name, and they charged them not to teach nor preach in that Name and sent them out.

They went back to their own company and told the story.

Then we have that remarkable prayer in which they said:

"And now, Lord, look upon their threatenings: and grant unto Thy servants to speak Thy Word with all boldness, while Thou stretchest forth Thy hand to heal; and that signs and wonders may be done through the Name of Thy Holy Child Jesus." Acts 4:29-30.

The disciples now expected that signs and wonders were to follow the preaching in the Name of Jesus.

"And the place was shaken where they were, and they were all filled with the Holy Spirit and spake the Word of God with boldness." Acts 4:31.

"And by the hands of the apostles were many signs and wonders wrought among the people. * * * And there came together the multitude from the cities round about Jerusalem, bringing sick folk and them that were vexed with unclean spirits: and they were healed every one." Acts 5:12, 16.

Jail Doors Were Opened

They were arrested again and put in a ward but the angel of the Lord opened the prison and told them to go and stand in the temple and preach all the words of this Life.

In the morning they were brought before the Council and the High Priest asked them, saying:

"We strictly charged you not to teach in this Name, and behold you have filled Jerusalem with your teaching and intend to bring this man's blood upon us." Acts 5:28.

Then came one of the most dramatic events in the Early Church: when the Council was divided and the power of God was so manifest among the people,—Gamaliel warned them not to touch them—said they might find themselves fighting against God.

But in the face of this, they beat the disciples, and charged them not to speak in the Name of Jesus and let them go.

"They departed from the presence of the Council, rejoicing that they were counted worthy to suffer dishonor for the Name." Acts 5:41.

No student can read this section of the Book of Acts without being impressed with the large place the Name of Jesus held in the Early Church.

Following the death of Stephen and the preaching of the Word by Philip in Samaria, we come to this significant statement.

"But when they believed Philip preaching good tidings concerning the kingdom of God and the Name of Jesus Christ, they were baptized, both men and women." Acts 8:12.

He not only preached the kingdom but he preached the Name of Jesus.

It seems that the Early Church devoted the time to instructing the people in regard to the use of the Name of Jesus.

They must have understood that they had what we would call today a legal Right to use the Name of Jesus.

The Name for Healing

They used it in connection with the sick; it would seem that they did not pray for the sick especially but that they laid their hands upon them in Jesus' Name, or as at the Beautiful Gate, they said, "In the Name of Jesus Christ of Nazareth, rise and walk."

At Paul's conversion in Acts 9:15-16 where God is sending Ananias to baptize Paul, He says this:

"For he is a chosen vessel unto Me, to bear My Name before the Gentiles and kings, and the children of Israel: for I will show him how many things he must suffer for My Name's sake."

That Name of Jesus was the battle axe in the ministry of Paul.

That Name was in the hands of Paul what the rod was in the hand of Moses.

If the Egyptians could have stolen that rod, they would have stripped Moses of his weapon.

Now, if the Gentiles and Jews could stop the Church from using the Name of Jesus, they would rob the Church of its supernatural power, and like Sampson when his hair was cut, they would be common men.

The Modern Church, having lost the power of the Name of Jesus, is reduced to the position of the shorn Sampson.

In Acts 9:27-29, we read:

"But Barnabas took him, and brought him to the apostles, and declared unto them how he had seen the Lord in the way, and that He had spoken to him, and how at Damascus he had preached boldly in the Name of Jesus. And he was with them, going in and out of Jerusalem preaching boldly in the Name of the Lord."

That means more than simply preaching the Gospel, as we understand it today.

Again, in the Council at Jerusalem, as recorded in Acts 15:14, James said:

"Brethren, hearken unto me: Symeon hath rehearsed how God first visited the Gentiles, to take out of them a people for His Name."

A People Gathered About the Name

The Gentile Church is a people taken out of the world unto the Name of Jesus, and we are a people who are gathered about the Name—when we meet as an assembly or a church, we are gathered about the Name of Jesus.

It is a supernatural body, clothed with supernatural power, gathered about a supernatural Name.

The Lord have mercy upon us! How we have fallen from our high estate.

One can go into the average church or assembly and hear men and women pleading with God for faith, bemoaning their weakness, confessing their inability to meet the crisis of the hour, when if they only knew the truth, they would gather about the Name of Jesus—this mighty Name that has enwrapped within it the Omnipotence of God, the power of Him Who bore it, and they know it not!

Oh, if they only knew how to turn on the switch and receive the light, and glory, and might of Omnipotence which is at their disposal.

In Acts 16:16-18 we have a striking illustration of the use of the Name:

"And it came to pass, as we were going to the place of prayer, that a certain maid having a spirit of divination met us, who brought her masters much gain by sooth-saying. The same following after Paul and us cried out, saying, These men are servants of the Most High God, who proclaim unto you the way of salvation. And this she did for many days. But Paul being sore troubled, turned and said to the spirit, I charge thee in the Name of Jesus Christ to come out of her. And it came out that very hour."

The girl was delivered, the apostles arrested; then came the mighty miracle of the opening of the jail at Philippi when the jailer fell trembling at the feet of Paul and Silas crying, "What shall we do to be saved?"

They answered, "Believe on the Lord Jesus, and thou shalt be saved."

This same Name that had liberated the girl from the power of the demon in the afternoon now has led this man into sonship privileges in the family of God.

The Name of Jesus meant more to the Early Church than it does to us; it had a place in their ministry that we do not give it in these days.

Have we anything to take its place?

They tell us that education will take its place; that the Church no longer needs the supernatural power of God.

They reason thus: That we have outgrown the teaching of the Holy Spirit and that the wisdom of man is to take the place of the power of the Name of Christ; that that Name has been stripped of its power because we through our colleges, universities, and our great intellectual development have outgrown God, and we can perform mental miracles so that God's physical miracles are unnecessary.

Shame upon us!

We have become an Apostate Church; we are groveling in the dust; we are held in bondage to our ignorance.

Israel when carried into captivity by the Babylonians is typical of the Church that has been carried into a Babylonish captivity by the world forces.

Nothing but a Supernatural God will ever deliver us!

How little we realize that our vain preaching and our vain writing are simply the laughing stock of the Enemy.

One mighty miracle today in the Name of Jesus Christ is worth more than a hundred modernistic sermons that are being preached in many churches.

Has God Lost His Power?

Has Jesus gone out of business?

Have we any record anywhere that God said the Name of Jesus is no longer needed?

That colleges, universities, and Scholasticism will take its place?

Let us read of another striking event in Acts 19:11-17:

"God wrought special miracles by the hands of Paul: insomuch that unto the sick were carried away from his body handkerchiefs or aprons, and the diseases departed from them, and the evil spirits went out. But certain also of the strolling Jews, exorcists, took upon themselves to speak over them that had the evil spirits, the Name of the Lord Jesus, saying, I adjure you by Jesus Whom Paul preacheth. And there were seven sons of one Sceva, a Jew, a chief priest, who did this. And the evil spirit answered and said unto them, Jesus I know, and Paul I know; but who are ye? And the man in whom the evil spirit was leaped on them, and mastered both of them, and prevailed against them, so that they fled out of that house, naked and wounded. And this became known to all, both Jews and Greeks, that dwelt at Ephesus; and fear fell upon them all, and the Name of the Lord Jesus was magnified."

Paul's ministry in the Name of Jesus was so outstanding, the miracles so pronounced, that even wicked men, sorcerers, attempted to use it; and that Name, through the mighty things that were wrought, was glorified in Ephesus.

Would that the Name of Jesus could be so glorified today in the churches and assemblies!

It would be if the believers knew their legal Rights and knew how to enjoy them.

In Acts 26:9 Paul in his defense says:

"I verily thought within myself that I ought to do many things contrary to the Name of Jesus of Nazareth."

Notice the place that Paul gives the Name in this Scripture—that he thought he ought to do many things contrary to the Name!

If we were to draw a conclusion from the use and place of the Name in the Book of Acts, what would we say?

The Name of Jesus actually took the place of the Ascended Lord; wherever Jesus would have been glorified by His personal presence, that Name took His place.

May the Lord open our blinded eyes!

That Name has lost none of its authority, none of its power, and the effort to rob us of some of the major portions of Scripture by a false dispensational division of Scripture fails utterly; for in Paul's ministry with the Gentiles and his epistles to the Gentiles, he gives the Name of Jesus a place that absolutely refutes the entire teaching of those who would put the power of the Name of Jesus over into the kingdom period.

No! The Name of Jesus belongs to us NOW.

It is our legal Right; that Name belongs to us.

How rich would be the Church today in power, and experience, and grace, if She knew Her privileges and arose in that Name and dared take them!

Chapter X

THE NAME IN THE EPISTLES

THE use of the Name in the Epistles is very illuminating.

"Unto the Church of God which is at Corinth, even them that are sanctified in Christ Jesus, called saints with all that call upon the Name of our Lord Jesus Christ in every place, their Lord and ours." 1 Cor. 1:2.

"With all that call upon the Name."

In those early days, the believers knew the value and place and authority of that Name—they appreciated it.

They walked and lived in the conscious freshness of the power of the Name of Jesus.

When they made an appeal to the brethren, they used language like this:

"Now, I beseech you, brethren, through the Name of our Lord Jesus Christ, that ye all speak the same thing, that there be no division among you."

Their appeal was in the Name of Jesus.

In I Cor. 5:4 we read, "In the Name of our Lord Jesus Christ, ye being gathered together."

Here, the Church is facing an internal trouble—one of the young men has committed a very grave misdemeanor.

And Paul tells them that when they have gathered together in the Name of the Lord Jesus Christ, they are to deliver such an one over to Satan for the destruction of the flesh, that the spirit may be saved in the day of Christ Jesus.

That Name had the power of Life and of Death in those days.

"And such were some of you: but ye were washed, but ye were sanctified, but ye were justified in the Name of the Lord Jesus Christ, and in the Spirit of our God." 1 Cor. 6:11.

Here, they are washed, sanctified, justified in that Name.

The farther you go in the Epistles, the more deeply you are impressed with the power, and dignity, and grace of God vested in that Name.

"Giving thanks always for all things in the Name of our Lord Jesus Christ to God, even the Father." Eph. 5:20.

Even our praises and our worship cannot go to God direct: they must come in the Name of our Lord Jesus Christ.

That does not hinder us from worshipping and praising Jesus Himself but when we praise the Father, it must be done in the Name of our Lord Jesus Christ.

"Wherefore also God highly exalted Him, and gave unto

Him the Name which is above every name; that at the Name of Jesus every knee should bow, of beings in heaven and beings on earth and beings under the earth, and that every tongue should confess that Jesus Christ is Lord, to the glory of God the Father." Philippians 2:9-11.

God has highly exalted the Name of Jesus in the three worlds—every knee bows; all the angelic beings bow before the Name of this Wonder Man Jesus.

No Name is so great, no Name has so many glories attached to it as the Name of Jesus.

On earth the Name of Jesus has steadily grown from the day when He lay an infant in the manger, and Mary looking upon Him remembered what the angels had said: "And His Name shall be called Jesus, for it is He Who shall save His people from their sins."

From the cradle with its prophecy, to the cross with its tragedy, and sweeping down through the ages, that Name has steadily grown until today, the Jew, the Gentile, and heathen of all lands are compelled to recognize that Name.

No man writes a deed in Christian Lands who does not honor the Name of Jesus. The date on that document, showing the year of our Lord (A. D.) must be written.

The Lord has so arranged it that everyone regardless of his belief must acknowledge the birth of Christ every time he dates a letter.

Wherever that Name has become known, honored, and venerated, habitations have changed to homes; the mother's position from that of a slave to that of the honored queen, girlhood from being despised to being honored and loved.

Wherever that Name is honored, educational institutions spring up, inventions, scientific investigation, and discoveries are fostered.

This Name that men have ignored and trampled upon during this dispensation will be the Name that will fill the hearts of wicked men with fear.

Do All Things in the Name

"And whatsoever ye do, in word or in deed, do all in the Name of the Lord Jesus, giving thanks to God the Father through Him." Col. 3:17.

In Ephesians, He told us when we worshipped the Father, it must be through the Name, but now, "whatsoever ye do in word or in deed, all must be done in the Name."

This ends the controversy in regard to praying to Jesus.

This gives Jesus His position; this exalts the Name in our daily life.

Whatsoever we do in word or in deed must be done in that Name, and in that Name only.

In 2 Thess. 1:11-12 we have another view of this: "To which end we also pray always for you that our God may count you worthy of your calling, and fulfill every desire of goodness and every work of faith, with power; that the Name of our Lord Jesus may be glorified in you, and ye in Him."

This sets forth more clearly perhaps, than any other Scripture we have used, the place of the Name in our daily life and ministry; that this Name may be glorified in our lives, and glorified through our ministry.

How could it be glorified more than by using it as the Early Church used it?

"Now, we command you, brethren, in the Name of our Lord Jesus Christ, that ye withdraw yourselves from every brother that walketh disorderly, and not after the tradition which they received of us." 2 Thess. 3:6.

Here, Paul commands the Church, in the Name of the Lord Jesus, to withdraw from every brother that walks disorderly.

How mighty that Name must have been in the mind of the Early Church!

"Through Him, then, let us offer up a sacrifice of praise to God continually, that is, the fruit of lips which make confession to His Name." Heb. 13:15.

Their public testimony was a confession of that Name.

I can understand now what it means in Acts 8: where it speaks of Philip preaching the kingdom of God and the Name of Jesus.

They preached the Name; they heralded the power, might, and wonder of that Name.

They appreciated what the promise of Jesus meant when He said, "Hitherto, ye have asked nothing in my Name."

They went out and suffered for the Name.

I understand more clearly how the Jews felt when they forbade the disciples preaching any more in that Name.

Afterwards, when the disciples were arrested, they said, "Did we not straightway forbid you preaching in this Name, and you have filled Jerusalem with it."

They knew its value, they lived in the freshness of its power, and those Jews knew its power too.

In James 2:7 we read, "Do not they blaspheme the honorable Name by which ye are called?"

James called it "that honorable Name.'"

The Name that had wrought such mighty things through all the country was looked up to with honor, respect, and love.

"Is any among you sick? Let him call for the elders of the Church; and let them pray over him, anointing him with oil in the Name of the Lord." James 5:14.

The sick were anointed in that Name for their healing.

47

"If ye are reproached for the Name of Christ, blessed are ye." 1 Pet. 4:14.

They gladly bore the reproach of that Name.

You can see very clearly that the Name of Jesus held a position in the front rank of their teaching; and whenever they entered a heathen village or city, they preached to them that Name as Philip preached it down at Samaria.

They let the people know that the Name of Jesus had power to heal the sick, cast out demons, perform miracles and prodigies—that their God was represented in that Name.

"I write unto you, My little children, because your sins are forgiven you for His Name's sake." 1 John 2:12.

Here, the Name is used in another sense, but with what a wealth of suggestiveness.

Sins are forgiven for His Name's sake—for the sake of that Name.

"And this is His commandment, that we should believe in the Name of His Son Jesus Christ and love one another." 1 John 3:23.

The command that we should believe in the Name is literally that we should believe the Name—the preposition "in" is not the Greek.

That we should believe the Name—believe it for what it stands—believe it for all that it means in the heart of the Father—that we believe the Name!

Reader, ask your heart this question, "Do I believe the Name of Jesus? What does it mean to my life?"

"These things have I written unto you that ye may know that ye have eternal life, even unto you that believe ON the Name of the Son of God." 1 John 5:13.

Here is a contrast between "in" and "on".

We believe ON the Name for salvation; we believe IN the Name for power in service.

Our position as believers in Christ gives us a legal right to pray in the Name of Jesus and take out of that Name the wealth of love, and riches, and grace, and salvation, and redemption that belongs to us.

We see by the teachings in the Epistles what Jesus meant when He gave the great promise of the use of His Name.

The Name of Jesus became the center around which everything was builded in their missionary activities.

They lived, and wrought, and praised in that Name.

That Name meant food and raiment; it meant deliverance from the hand of their enemies—it meant power over demons and diseases; it meant worship, and praise, and access to God.

Enwrapped in that mighty Name is the invisible power and miracle working might of the Church of Jesus Christ today.

Chapter XI

THE NAME IN DAILY CONFLICT

N THIS Name lies the very essence of Christianity; it is the one thing which differentiates it from all other religions.

It is the one Name that challenges an adjective to qualify it.

While here in the flesh, Jesus was the all-powerful One; God always heard His prayers, and permitted Him to use Omnipotence as He willed.

Before He went away, He promised that this same Right to use the Omnipotence of God should be left on earth, available to man.

He told the disciples not to leave Jerusalem until they were endued or clothed with power from on high.

The Holy Spirit was to come into them and enable them to use His Name in the will of God, so that it would be as though Christ were again in the flesh exercising this Divine power, only in a larger sense, because there will be so many using His Name.

Filled with the Spirit, they preached in this Name with awful power.

The sick were healed, demons were cast out, and the dead were raised; in this Name a serpent's bite became the means of the inhabitants of a whole island receiving Jesus Christ as their Saviour.

In this Name came the Gift of Tongues which enabled all nations on the Day of Pentecost to hear the glad tidings of remission of sins.

He Willed Us His Name

All this was in fulfillment of the words spoken by Jesus Christ before His ascension.

"In My Name shall they cast out demons; they shall speak with new tongues; they shall take up serpents, and if they drink any deadly thing it shall in no wise harm them; they shall lay hands on the sick and they shall recover."

This power was not in the Holy Spirit, but in the Spirit's enabling the disciples to use the Name of the Lord Jesus Christ, the Son of God.

All power is in the Name of the risen Man Christ Jesus Who is seated at the Father's right hand in the heavens.

The power is not in fasting or consecration, not in long prayers, but it is in the simple Name of Jesus of Nazareth, the Son of God.

Men are seeking power—they call it Pentecostal power—

k it in all directions but the right one; it is in the
seek it there.

u learn to use the Name according to the Word, in the
power of the Spirit, you have the secret which shook the world
through the apostles.

How to Use His Name

You must be a scriptural believer, a child of God, obedient
to the Word.

You must come to God, the Father, through Christ.

Don't pray to Jesus; don't pray to the Holy Spirit; never
ask for the SAKE of Jesus—always pray in His Name.

Be definite; don't insult the Father by indefinite ramblings,
but ask for what you want.

Approach the Father as a son—not as a slave or servant;
you are His child, He is your loving Father; He loves you, you
love Him and are free and happy in His presence.

Your chief desire is that He may receive glory so talk plainly
with Him, open your heart, lay your desire before His eyes
and make your case clear; let Him see that it is for His glory
and the good of others.

Then clinch it by making your worthy claim in the Name
of His Son Who sits at His right hand, reminding Him of His
promise, "Whatsoever you ask the Father IN MY NAME, He
will give it you."

The Divine Advocate

Now, you have a clear case; the Lord Jesus is there to
present your claim.

You have, by asking in His Name, made Christ your Advocate, and now the case belongs to Him.

Your humble, simple prayer, made in this scriptural way,
becomes Christ's prayer at God's right hand; you drop out of
the question and the mighty Advocate takes your case.

This shows us what power we have up there and down
here.

Be fearless after this; challenge your mountain in that all-
sufficient Name; it must move.

Sin, sickness, circumstances, Satan—all must yield to that
Name.

Use this NAME though you tremble when you do it—it is
not you, but the power behind the Name; you do not need to
feel its power—you know it—and everything must flee at this
all-conquering Name.

"Hitherto ye have asked nothing in My Name; ask, and ye
shall receive, that your joy be made full."

The Simplicity of Prayer

This is one of the startling statements of the Gospel:

"Whatsoever ye shall ask the Father in My Name, that will I do."

Notice Jesus said, "You ask—and I will do it."

This is a most wonderful thing—prayer simplified.

"You do the asking," Jesus says, "and I will do the doing."

Jesus says all authority has been given unto Him in heaven and on earth.

Jesus' power is unlimited, and now He challenges you to do unlimited asking.

He is big enough to do anything you ask Him to do.

His authority is great enough to see that any request from you is honored.

For that unsaved friend, He says, "You ask for his salvation and I will do it."

It may be your church is cold and your pastor as bound as Lazarus in the grave clothes of convention, yet you ask and Jesus says, "I will do it."

He will warm the Church.

You ask for a revival—Jesus will "do it."

Jesus sits at the right hand of the Father and whatsoever you ask of the Father in His Almighty Name, He says, "I will do it."

That loved one is sick; ask for healing, and as surely as God is on His throne, so surely must He do it.

You ask for the finances for that undertaking for the Lord: your business is to ask; His business is to see that it is done.

Behind everything stand these words of Christ, "I will do it."

There is no reason for our weakness; there is no reason for our sickness.

There is no reason for a fruitless Church or ministry.

There is no reason for powerless lives.

You resolve your life into the service of asking—challenging the Omnipotence of the living, reigning Christ and He will take care of His end of the deal.

You are a partner with Him now; you need not write "limited" to this partnership, because His company is not limited: He is able to meet the demands; He is able to finance any undertaking.

The great and mighty Christ is willing for you to ask that He may give.

Weakness is a crime now, poverty of spirit a sin, all you need to do is ask and He will act.

How to Pray

Jesus tell us how to pray—"when ye pray, say, Our Father."

We are not to pray to Jesus.

That does not exclude the privilege of joy, and fellowship, and the communion with Him nor the praise and worship of Him, but when we have a special petition, our prayer shall be addressed to the Father in the Name of Jesus.

Not "for Jesus' sake" for that would mean to do it for Jesus' sake rather than for the sake of the one that needs it.

The prayer shall be addressed simply to Our Father, in Jesus' Name; that guarantees the Father's answer and Jesus' endorsement and intercession.

I know that the habit of praying to Jesus is very wide-spread, but if we want the truth and we desire to pray in such a manner that we can be sure of our answer, then we must obey the Scriptures and pray as they teach us.

You see Jesus' Name was to take the place of Jesus.

What the rod was in the hands of Moses, the Name of Jesus is in the hands of the weakest child of God.

It was not that Moses was great but that the rod was great.

It is not that the believer is great but that the Name of Jesus is great.

The use of that Name is promised to every believer and every believer has a right to lay hands on the sick in that Name.

The believer has a right to use it in every condition of life where the Father's presence and help are necessary.

The fact is that the Name of Jesus in the hands of every believer should be the same as though Jesus Himself were present and operating.

Jesus has given us a legal right to use His Name.

He has given to us the Power of Attorney and the Power of Attorney in the legal and business world is identical with the presence of the person who gave it.

It is just as though Jesus said, "When you pray in My Name, that gives Me an opportunity to begin to work, and in that way I may glorify My Father.

If you don't pray in My Name, you don't give Me an opportunity to manifest My power."

In this way, both the Father and the Son become vitally interested in the petition that we make.

You are praying to the Father and you are praying in the Name of His Son.

Chapter XII

CONTRAST OF SENSE KNOWLEDGE FAITH AND REVELATION FAITH

ENSE knowledge faith is based upon physical evidence. One believes in what they can see, hear or feel. We know that we have the Holy Spirit because we have had physical evidences to prove it.

Multitudes have taken this attitude and have been unhappily deceived. Had they based their confidence upon the Word of God regardless of all sense knowledge evidences, life would have been another thing for them.

Others when they have prayed for finances, have not believed the Word until they could see the evidences. As one said, "When I see the money, then I will believe the Word."

You see, that is not believing at all, because one needs not believe what they can see.

Faith is giving substance to things you cannot see, feel or hear.

One says, "I know that I am healed, because the pain is gone."

He did not say, "I know I am healed because the Word says, 'By His Stripes, I am healed'."

His faith was not in what God had said, but in what he could see, feel or hear.

These people give the Word a second place in their lives.

They give to their body, the home of the senses, the first place.

One says, "I know that I am saved, because I have repented of my sins. I have given up all of my bad habits."

Every one of these things that he claims for his salvation are things that he did himself. He has given no Scriptural evidence of his salvation. He has depended upon physical evidences rather than the Word of God.

After a while he makes the discovery that the evidences of the senses cannot satisfy the craving of the spirit.

Sense knowledge philosophy has gained control of the Church, but it cannot answer the cry of the human spirit.

The human spirit seeks God as the flower seeks the sun.

Basing our faith upon what we have done and counting more on experiences than upon the Word eventually leads us into darkness and doubt.

Acting on reason instead of the Word means to trust in man instead of God's Word.

"Cursed is the man that trusteth in man, that maketh flesh his arm."

Trusting in the faith of some other person is dangerous. We should trust in the Word of God ourselves.

Most people who are untaught in the Word are seeking for someone who can pray the prayer of faith for them. The prayer of faith may deliver temporarily, but unbelief will annul the effect of their prayer eventually.

It is having faith, believing in your own faith, trusting in the Word of God for yourself that will put you over. It is not talking about faith, or the need of faith, but it is resting implicitly in the living Word.

The prayer for faith will necessarily be a prayer of unbelief. Consequently, there can be no answer for it. Then your praying for faith is simply unbelief attempting to get what the Word alone can give.

You understand that simple confidence in the Word is never sensible to the man who lives in the realm of the senses, for they only believe what they can see, hear or understand.

Faith is giving substance to things that sense knowledge cannot understand or see.

It lifts one out of the realm of the senses into the realm of the recreated human spirit.

Faith is always limited, as it was with Martha and Thomas. Martha said, "His body decayeth."

Thomas said. "Unless I call see the wounds and put my fingers into the wounds, I will not believe."

This kind of faith is commended by our modern religious leaders, but this is not the faith mentioned by Jesus or by the writers of the New Testament.

We have been trained to believe in the skill of men. We have more confidence in the surgeon than we have in the Word and because of that, we see little manifestations of the real faith in the Living Word, for the skill of man, and what we call science, has taken the place of the Word in the hearts of the people. Their faith is in man and they honor man with their lips.

Their confession is not that the Word of God is true, but that man and his words are true. You see, they honor God with their lips, but they trust in the arm of flesh with their hearts.

Mental Assent

This assenting to the fact that God cannot fail to help us at a crisis period and yet, at the same time, turning to the world for assistance is a dangerous symptom.

Mental assent is one of the most dangerous of the enemies of a life of faith. It looks and sounds so religious. It will go so far as to say, "I believe in the verbal inspiration of the Bible. I am contending for the faith once delivered to the saints." Yet, they dare not act on the Word; they do not give it its place, they merely talk about its integrity.

The Mental Assenter is in the gravest of danger. He is where God cannot reach him; but where Satan can enter into his inner counsel. He therefore loses his rights and privileges in Christ.

Acting On the Word

The greatest battle that any child of God will ever fight is the battle of Faith.

We often wonder why it is so hard to believe God.

The reason is that we are surrounded by an antagonistic atmosphere that is presided over by the enemy of all righteousness, we live in his unreal world; we are surrounded by currents of unbelief so subtle that almost one does not realize them, and so resistless that only a few ever rise above them.

To believe in God for finances is a continual struggle against the materialistic currents that buffet us.

To believe in Christ for victory over sin is a battle during every hour of consciousness, with the spiritual hosts of darkness.

To believe in God for the physical body when one is ill is to put up a battle against the centuries of trust in medicine.

So it is not at all strange that so many break down in their faith-life and we should not be harsh or censorious against those who fail.

Faith and Believing

Faith is a noun; Believe is a verb—an analysis of these two words may help you in trusting the Lord.

Believing, being a verb, is an action word—it really means "taking"; to believe in a Biblical sense means "to take", "to grasp."

To believe Jesus means to take Jesus for all that the Scriptures declare Him to be.

To believe on Christ as a Saviour means to take Christ as a Saviour; to believe in Christ as a healer means to take Him as your healer and recognize Him as your healer.

Believing is an act of the will; when I believe, I have acted—having acted, I have reached what is called Faith.

Faith is a noun.

I take a step—having taken the step, I have arrived.

Arriving is Faith.

To believe, then, is to act on the Word of God. Faith is action. Doubting is refusing to act on the Word.

There are two kinds of Unbelief: first, a refusing to act on the knowledge of the Word that we have.

This can be called unpersuadableness—we refuse to be persuaded to act on what we know to be true; we refuse to act in the light of knowledge.

The other kind of Unbelief arises from lack of knowledge of the Word.

We do not know; hence, we cannot act.

We do not understand; hence, we are afraid to act.

We would act, but we do not know how to act.

The cure for this is knowledge; the cure for the other is obedience.

Chapter XIII

THE NAME IN BAPTISM

 HEN a Believer is baptized into the Name of the Lord Jesus, He puts on Christ, as Paul tells us in Galatians 3:27.

"For as many of you as were baptized into Christ, did put on Christ."

Baptism in this sense, is equivalent to marriage.

When the wife puts on marriage she takes her husband's name and enters into her husband's possessions and has legal rights in his home.

So when the believer is baptized into the Name of the Lord Jesus, he puts on the Name of the Lord Jesus.

He not only puts on the Name, but he takes his legal rights and privileges in Christ.

When we are baptized into the Name of the Father, it gives us the place of a child and all the privileges of a child, all the inheritance and wealth of the child.

We are baptized into the protection and care and fellowship of the God of the universe as our Father—.

We take on all that union means.

We have the standing of a Son, the privilege of a Son, the responsibilities of a Son.

We have become by that baptism a joint heir with Jesus, and an heir of God.

We have entered into the wealth of an inheritance from the God of the universe.

When we are baptized into the Name of the Holy Spirit, we are baptized into the Name, wealth, power, wisdom and glory of God's representatives on the earth—all the Spirit has we are baptized into.

We have become a fellowshipper of His grace, His tenderness, His wisdom, His ability, His power, His life.

So when we are baptized into the Name of the Lord Jesus, all that that Name stands for in heaven is ours; all the mighty victories that Jesus won in His death, and resurrection are ours.

What does it mean to be baptized into the Name?

Take this scripture: "Baptizing them into the Name of the Father, and into the Name of the Son, and into the Name of the Holy Spirit."

Spiritually it means this if it means anything:

That we are baptized into all that Name means in the Plan of Redemption—we are baptized into the Finished work of Christ.

Christ Our Fullness

Of His fullness we have received, and in Him we are full or complete.

All the grace that was manifest in Christ enwraps us, enfolds us—we are in it.

All the perfections and beauties in the character and life of Jesus are ours.

Paul says: "Ye are complete in Him."

It means in the mind of Paul that the completeness, the fullness, the perfection of Christ was all reckoned unto us.

Paul said: "As many as have been baptized into Christ have put on Christ."

Think of the responsibilities attached to it! Think of the glories enwrapped in it! Think of the blessings that accrue from it!

To be baptized into the Name of Christ, and the putting on of Christ, bearing the Name of Christ is the greatest honor that heaven can confer upon a human.

What mighty works can be wrought through the Holy Child Jesus!

The Lord lifts us up—the Lord enables us—by His grace, to enter into our inheritance and to assume our responsibilities in His wonderful family!

He won no victory and He won no triumph in His substitutionary work that was not for the benefit of the church.

Our Inheritance

All that Name stands for, the believer stands for in the presence of the Father.

You are baptized into the legal right to use the Name.

You are baptized into the legal privilege of that Name.

You are baptized into all the responsibilities of a Son—vested with prerogatives of that mighty Name.

God help us by the power of the Spirit to enter into the riches of our inheritance in Him.

When He said, "All authority is given unto me in heaven and on earth I send you out as heralds"—then that authority He had is ours; we stand as His representatives.

His righteousness is ours, His love is ours; all the graces that adorned His beautiful life are ours.

When we put on Christ in baptism, we are by His grace able to enjoy all the graces.

As believers, all these riches, all these graces are ours.

No special act on the part of God—no special act or preparation on our part: by faith, we accept Christ as our Saviour and Lord and when we did, all the wealth and riches in Christ Jesus became ours automatically.

We stand clothed in the rights, privileges, and powers of the Son of God.

A Three-fold Meaning

Rom. 6:4 "We were buried therefore with him through baptism into death: that like as Christ was raised from the dead through the glory of the Father, so we also might walk in newness of life."

Baptism has a three-fold significance.

First: It is the death and burial of the past.

Second: It is a resurrection into a new relationship.

Third: It is a union with the one in whose Name we have been baptized.

We are baptized into the Name of the Father.

This means sonship with all the privileges that come with a relationship of such a person as the Father-God.

It means that we have died to all our previous relationships—that from now on our life is dependent upon Him.

To be baptized into the Holy Spirit means that I have died to my past—my old relationships are severed—I am raised in Him, to live and walk in fellowship with Him.

His wisdom is to take the place of my ignorance; His strength is to take the place of my weakness; His goodness is to take the place of my failures.

In other words, I am so fully identified and so completely at one with Him that it can no longer be I that live but He that liveth His life in me.

Baptizing into the Name of the Lord Jesus Christ is even richer and fuller than either of these—it comprehends all that is in them with additions.

When I am baptized into Christ, I put on Christ.

I am now legally before the world, and before heaven a Christ—ian.

Baptism in this sense is equivalent to marriage.

When the wife puts on marriage she takes her husband's name and enters into her husband's possessions and has legal rights in her husband's home.

When the believer is baptized into the Name of Christ, he puts on all that is in Christ.

He not only puts on the Name but takes his legal Rights and privileges in Christ.

When a wife is married into the name of the husband, she is married into his wealth, honor, and glory and becomes identified with him in all that he was or ever will be.

So when we are baptized into the Name of the Lord Jesus, we are baptized into all that Name stands for—all its wealth, all its honor—all its power—all its past, present and future glory.

All that that Name stands for in heaven is ours; all the mighty victories He won in His death, suffering, and conquest in hell and His resurrection are ours.

All, All, Is Ours

He won no victory, He won no triumph in His substitutionary work that was not for the benefit of those united to Him in baptism.

All that Name stands for before the Father belongs to the believer.

We are baptized into the Legal Right to use the Name, into the Legal Privileges of that Name, into all the responsibility of a son, vested with the prerogatives of that mighty Name.

When He said, "All authority is given unto Me in heaven and in earth," and, "I send you out as heralds," then that authority He had is ours—we stand as His representatives—we go out into this world bearing His Name.

Thus instead of our bearing the Name, the Name actually bears and succors us.

We are baptized into His righteousness, into His resurrection, power, and glory.

Now, His righteousness is ours; His grace is ours; His love is ours; His power is ours; yes, He Himself is ours.

How rich we are!

Now to use this Name does not require any special or unusual Faith because it is ours.

As believers, all the riches and graces are ours—no special act on the part of God—no special preparation on our part is necessary when some great crisis arises—that Name is ours, given to us legally to use against the host of God's enemies, and we stand clothed in the Rights, privileges, and powers of the sons of God.

We do not have to exercise any conscious Faith—all we have to do is to use the Name.

The heart can hardly take it in, that when we were baptized into that Name, we were baptized into the fullness, the completeness, the perfections of Jesus Christ.

That of His Fullness have we all received and grace upon grace.

Chapter XIV

IDENTIFICATION WITH CHRIST

HE glorious fact of our Identification with Christ is one of the richest facts in the whole Plan of Redemption.

We were crucified with Christ—we were nailed to the cross with Him, in the mind of God.

As He was stripped naked and hung there in His shame and disgrace, so we also, were stripped naked and hung there, for He took our place on the cross.

We died with Christ, as He died.

As He died to sin, so we died to sin.

As He died to Satan's rule, so we died to it.

As He died to sickness and disease, we died.

We were buried together with Him as He went down into the place of suffering and paid the penalty of our sins and union with Satan.

As He put off from Himself the forces of darkness and sin, the sickness and diseases of man, so we put them off in Him—we left them there.

We were raised together with Christ.

He was raised up by the glory of the Father, when He had satisfied the claims of Justice, and had met our great enemy Satan and His army in the dark regions of hell and conquered them.

He then was made alive in spirit, and justified in spirit.

Then, He arose; and we rose with Him.

He was raised up because God justified Him, and He could not be held longer, by death and hell.

When He was justified, we were justified in Him.

When He was healed of death, we were healed in Him.

When He conquered sickness and disease, so also did we, in Him.

To all who are in Christ, disease is a conquered foe.

We are seated with Christ at the Right Hand of God,—in the highest place of power in the Universe.

Identified with Him in suffering and shame, and in glory.

Law of Identification

He has conquered death, hell, and the grave.

He has risen from the conquest of our enemies a Victor.

We were identified with Him in that conquest.

We died with Him, we suffered with Him, and when He put off from Himself the principalities and powers, and conquered Satan, paralyzing his death-dealing power, we were identified with Him.

When He rose from among the dead and stood triumphant over death, hell, Satan and disease, and the grave, we stood with Him.

Now, He gives to us the use of the Name that was conferred upon Him when He had accomplished this mighty work in satisfying the claims of justice, defeating Satan, and meeting the needs of humanity.

He gives to us that Name which is above every Name—the Name to which every knee shall bow and every tongue confess in the three worlds.

In His great grace He gave us the use of that Name; He gave us a legal right to use it.

He died as our representative; now we live as His representatives.

That Name represents all that He was or is, all that He ever did or will do.

When, by a thorough understanding of this, we have been ushered into this faith realm, and we use that Name intelligently, all that Name means in heaven, it will mean to us.

He has put absolutely no limitation upon our use of that Name.

The only question is: "Do I understand what God means in giving me the use of that Name?"

We are not to use it as the heathen use their fetishes, but we are to use it in a business sense, the legal sense of power of attorney.

We use His Name representatively.

The sick and afflicted come to us, and healing virtue that is in Christ—that is in His finished work, is available to the sick one in that Name.

Then—it is not healing through Christ;—that Name becomes Christ, the healer.

A Living Fact

When Jesus was crucified, He took my place as a sinner.

He bore my sins in his body on the tree; He bore my shame that came through my union with Satan; He bore my diseases that Satan had put upon me; He bore my judgment which was mine, because of my union with God's enemy.

When He died, He carried all this off into the land of Forgetfulness and He rose because He had put all this away.

He not only put my sin away, my shame and my diseases, but He put me away—the old me—me, the sinner.

He put my sin nature away.

He put my infirmities away along with my sin, sicknesses, and diseases, so that now I stand with Him and in Him as free from them as He was free when He rose.

A New Creation

His justification is my justification; His righteousness is my righteousness; His health is my health; His freedom from Satan's dominion is my freedom; His freedom from condemnation, is my freedom from condemnation; His freedom from infirmities, is my freedom from infirmities; for in Him I enjoy all that He did and all that He now is.

All that He did, He did for me.

Let me state it again:

Jesus, My Substitute

If He bore my sins, I do not need to bear them; If He bore my sin nature, I do not need to bear it; If He bore my infirmities, I do not need to carry them;—If I DO bear them, then He died for naught.

So when I accepted Him as my Saviour, confessed Him as my Lord, and was baptized into His Name, I was baptized into His standing before the Father.

I was baptized into His righteousness that He wrought; I was baptized into His justification; baptized into His health for the body, soul and spirit; I was baptized into the victory that He had won over Satan; I was baptized into all He means to the Father, for He died representatively for me; and now, He reigns up there, representatively for me.

As He is my representative up there, now, I am His representative here in the earth.

He has put me, and mine, and all the sin, that was in me, away, and He has given me all that was His: all that He did, all that He was, so that "as He is now, so am I in this world."

The Struggle Is Over

It does not require any faith on my part to enjoy this, because He gave it to me; it is mine, and what is mine I do not have to have faith to obtain, for I have already obtained it; I am in possession of it.

All I need to do is praise Him for it, and when I praise Him and thank Him for it, then the thing becomes operative in my life.

So now, I stand before God and the angels—yes, and before Satan—clothed in Christ, hidden in Christ, enwrapped in Christ.

Think what it means! His Name is the Name of the Conqueror, and I am baptized into this Name, and bear this Name; I bear the Name of the Conqueror.

"For as many as were baptized into Christ have put on Christ."

I have put on Christ; Christ tabernacles Himself over me.

"It is no longer I then that live but Christ liveth in me."

"Wherefore, if any man be in Christ, he is a new creature."

Then, I am a new creature, and that new creature is seated with Christ.

"Old things have passed away."

The old things of weakness, the old things of failure, the old things of impotence, the old things of unbelief, are passed away while the new things of faith, the new things of life, the new things of health for body, soul, and spirit are mine.

I live in the new realm where the new things are a reality.

"And that life I now live, I live by faith in the Son of God Who loved me and gave Himself up for me."

I do not have to TAKE this position; I am in this position.

I do not have to struggle for it, believe for it, die daily for it, for I am in it—it is mine. Mine because when I was born again, and baptized into the Name of the Lord Jesus, I was born into it, I was baptized into it, and I am in it. Hallelujah!

This gives me the undisputed Right to the use of His Name and all that Name stands for in Earth, Heaven, and Hell.

Prayer Battle

If planning to use the Name of Jesus in prayer battles, one needs to know the power invested in that Name which God esteems above every Name.

That Name stands for us as Jesus stands for us.

When one really prays in that Name intelligently, scripturally, and in the Will of God, it is as though Christ Himself, prayed.

There is no force, might, or authority in earth, air, or hell that can prevent its answer: it simply must come to pass.

In your own integrity, in your rights, privileges, and authority you approach your mountain, you command it in that Name, "Up, hurl yourself into the sea."

The mountain cannot help it. You cannot help it. All hell cannot help it. It simply must go.

Back of your command lies God's integrity, His omnipotence, and Christ's unlimited power, all at your disposal.

Stand in the Name

The hosts of hell may assault you, but you meet them in that Name that once spread consternation through hell, when He put, "to naught him that had the authority of death, that is the devil." Hebrews 2:14.

Satan dares not face the warrior who is clothed in Christ's righteousness, and who knows the power of that mighty Name.

Mark 11:23 "Whosoever shall say unto this mountain, Be thou taken up and cast into the sea and shall not doubt in his heart, but shall believe that what he saith cometh to pass; he shall have it."

You think your mountain is large, the sea at a great distance, your own faith small; well, all this may be true, but you have confidence in that Name even if you have not in your own faith.

So, in that great Name command the mountain to go—not in your faith, but in that Name. It will go. It must go!

It is not the quantity of faith, but the place where it is centered.

If you ask in that Name, you are a victor from this hour, whether it concerns money, health, or souls, you cannot fail.

The Mighty Name that heads up all the power of the Universe says so, and it must be so.

God's Will

An unswerving, unconquerable will knows no defeat.

You come to your mountain, you know its power, its greatness; you have compassed it more than seven days; you have faced it perhaps for a long period, but the battle must be fought today.

You know you are in His will.

So now you will this mountain to go; your will becomes His will; your command, His command.

You say, "In the Name of Jesus I command you to go."

That makes Jesus say it, and when He says it, that makes the Father say it.

Standing back of you are the union of the Trinity and the power of the Universe.

Your will and God's will are allied against the enemy.

They are now identical.

Through you God is able to fight His enemies.

Through you He can act.

Through you He can use His power as He wills to use it.

You hurl that matchless Name of His Son against the hosts of hell, and they will fly in confusion.

You walk among men, the God-man—a man of God.

God has put Himself in your hands and says, "Use my Will, Name, Word and Power" and your mountain becomes a plain.

Your opponents have to fight God.

The battle is His.

It is His honor now, that is assailed.

He fights; men tremble, and fall to rise no more.

Gird Yourself With the Name

As the hosts of evil come against you, you gather up your entire moral, mental, and spiritual energy, and in the Name of Christ you throw yourself against them.

You are a part of that Name as you are a part of God, so your victory must be complete.

You are identified in Christ in all He is, was, or will be.

Your enemy may be stubborn and resist you, but your will is set,—you are going to win, and you literally charge on the enemy in that all-conquering Name.

The enemy may stand for a time, but he must yield; it takes a strong will to hold us quiet in some places, but God can make our wills strong enough to do it.

Persistence

You know, and have set your WILL to do the will of God; now, push your way up through every obstacle the enemy may place in your way.

Gather up all there is in you, and drive your shrinking, halting flesh into the briars.

It must go—shout your command and stand to it until you are obeyed.

"If he shrink back, my soul hath no pleasure in him," has spurred me over many a rough place, held me true in some awful hours.

If you have taken hold of the plow, hold on until the field is finished.

These weak-kneed men and women are a sad army.

Look up to that mountain; it is yours!

"Every place where your foot shall tread I have given it to you for an INHERITANCE."

This blessed, inspiring promise greeted Israel as they faced the Promised Land. Foot-prints meant possession, but it must be their own foot-prints.

Our Joshua gives us the same incentive for conquest.

Every promise in the New Testament that we put our feet upon is ours.

The rich plain of healing is yours if you will simply put your foot there.

The upland of spiritual power is yours, though Anak may live there; it is yours if you will but go against him and drive him out of his strongholds in the might of the Name.

All the blessed promises of the Old Book are yours, and why are ye so slack to go up and possess your land?

Between you and your possessions that huge mountain looms up.

Gather your forces, and in that all-sufficient Name, go against it.

Don't give up until the last enemy is conquered and is paying tribute to you.

The size of your inheritance depends upon how much land you have trodden under foot, really stood on, or walked over.

You can claim as many promises, (and hold them as your property), as you have tested and found true.

So march up to this mountain and make it yours.

Every lust and passion can be captured and made a soldier of the cross if you persevere with a will that will not be beaten or driven from the field.

Persistence is greater than genius.

Satan knows that you realize that your interests and God's are identified, and that God cannot see you fail without seeing Himself fail; and this He will not allow.

Then with a knowledge of your privileges, as a Son of God, and a will to have them for yourself and others, coupled with a persistent spirit that will not admit defeat, you can cast into the sea any mountain that stands before you.

Go in this thy might and God will get glory and you victory.

Chapter XV

MAN'S THREE-FOLD NATURE

AN is a three-fold being—body, soul, spirit.

Man's education should cover his whole being.

To train only the physical is to make a prize fighter.

To train only the mental is to make an intellectual anarchist.

To train only the spiritual is to make a fanatic.

But God planned to develop the whole man.

Man's spiritual nature is capable of culture that will enable him to know God and commune intelligently with Him.

It was God's dream that man should be His companion, so his spiritual faculties were originally attuned to the pitch of this dream.

Through the Fall, man was alienated from God.

His spiritual faculties were greatly impaired; yet, through Christ, this lost fellowship is restored.

The spiritual faculty in man is capable of marvelous development; yet our educational institutions fail to recognize its possibilities.

Our Realm

The supernatural realm is really the realm of the believer.

No one knows how much the mind and spirit can be developed.

If the body is kept in fine fettle, there is almost no limitation to man's mental and spiritual development.

We have been slow to come to a realization that man is spirit and that his spirit nature is his basic nature.

We have sought to educate him along intellectual lines, utterly ignoring the spiritual, so man is a self-seeking and self-centered being.

Thus man has lost his sense of relationship and responsibility toward God and man.

This makes him lawless—an anarchist.

We cannot ignore the spiritual side of man without magnifying the intellectual and physical; to do this without the restraint of the spirit is to unleash sex passions and give them dominance over the whole man.

Man must have fellowship for his spiritual nature.

There must be a culture and development of the spiritual nature to the point where it can enjoy fellowship with the Father God.

The heart or spirit of man craves the touch of the supernatural.

The love for the miraculous is in man.

The spirit of man cannot be analyzed or classified by the mind; it is above mind, as God is above the physical nature.

Man's intellect is ever conscious of supernatural forces about him that he cannot understand or interpret; perhaps, that is the reason why man longs to perform miracles.

The Soul Cry for Miracles

The curiosity for the miraculous is deep-seated in man.

Man was brought into being by a miracle-working God and man will ever yearn to work miracles.

The supernatural realm is really man's realm.

Sin has blinded us and has kept us from finding the secret door that will lead us back to our lost estate.

But the hunger is there, and the miracle is the way to bring man to God.

Is there a miracle element in Christianity today?

Did miracles end with the death of the disciples?

Are the so-called miracles that men claim to perform to-day fraudulent or purely psychic?

These are questions that we cannot ignore.

There has come a falling away on the part of the churches.

Modernism dominates the great religious forces of Christendom; its denial of the supernatural element in Christianity makes it simply an ethical religion.

On the other hand, we have those who are contending for an original, miraculous element in Christianity, but declaring that miracles ceased with the death of the apostles; that Christianity does not need the miraculous today to convince men of the Deity of Jesus.

Then we have a third group who claim miracles are still being performed; that the sick are healed, that prayers are answered, and that God is a living reality in the daily life of the believer.

We cannot ignore the amazing growth of Christian Science, Unity, New Thought, and Spiritism.

The people who are flocking to them are not the ignorant masses, but the most cultured and wealthy of the land, and their strongest appeal is the supernatural element of their so-called religions—the testimonies of healings by their followers are their strongest asset.

We cannot close our eyes to the fact that in many of our cities on the Pacific Coast, Mrs. Eddy has a stronger following today and a larger attendance at her churches than have the old line denominations; and the largest percentage of her followers have at one time been worshippers in the denominations—they have left them because they believe they are receiving more help from Mrs. Eddy's teaching than from the preachers.

They will tell you how they were healed and how they were helped in their spiritual life by this strange cult.

This is a libel upon the modern Church—it is not only a libel but a challenge.

What We Need

We have lost the supernatural element out of Christianity and we are clinging with trembling hands to a historical Christ that has no power to heal the sick and no ability to meet our daily needs.

The spirit of real evangelism is almost a thing of the past.

We have driven the miracle working Christ out of the Church; now we are driving the believers in miracles out of the Church.

We cannot blame the missions and non-conformist cults that are rising everywhere.

It is a protest of the people against the modern theological thought that dominates the Church.

Christian Science could not have grown to the place where it is dominating many of our large cities unless there had been a demand in the heart of the people for a supernatural religion.

The Pentecostal movement could not have risen with the Power that it has, had not the heart of the people been craving a new, fresh vision of Christ.

A dead orthodoxy has no resurrection power within it—no miracle working force back of it.

The people are putting up with extravagances and fanaticism in order that they may get a little touch of the supernatural God.

Cultured men and women will listen to uneducated preachers because the uneducated preacher in the dingy mission has faith in a living God.

When men tell us that we do not need miracles today—that education will take their place—they have not thought through on this subject.

No man can actually live and walk with the Man of Galilee without living in the realm of the miraculous.

Jesus is as much a miracle now as ever.

Man needs His miraculous touch now more than ever.

Nothing but a return to this God of Miracles will save our land and nation.

Is This True?

If a preacher has the reputation of acting on James 5:14 or Mark 16:18 he is disqualified for most of the denominational pulpits.

The Church is no longer in the grip of God, but under the sway of scholastic intolerance.

Our slogan should be "Back to the Living, Miracle Working Christ."

People want Him, so they crowd the building where he is allowed to act.

Jesus attracted the multitude by miracles.

Jesus will attract them today.

"He is the same yesterday, today, and forever."

We have three classes today.

First, those in whom the physical dominate.

These are governed by their passions, appetites and physical desires.

Second, those in whom the mind dominates.

In this class, we have the great financial, educational, social and political leaders.

A purely intellectual development makes man a dangerous asset to society; it develops his ego, his selfishness, and self-consciousness.

Third, those in whom the spirit dominates.

These are the great spiritual leaders of the Church today — men who are seeking to restore man to his original spiritual realm.

Three-Fold Development

There must be a three-fold education in order to make society sane, safe and progressive.

A purely intellectual attainment lacks balance, lacks the governing and discipline that the spiritual only can give.

This explains the crime wave that is sweeping over the land.

For two generations we have been developing the physical and mental at the expense of the spiritual.

Where children have no spiritual training in the home or in the school, and are not brought in contact with it in the Church, they develop unconsciously an abnormal individualism.

This is the basis of anarchy.

Every man becomes a law unto himself: the gratification of his desires, the carrying out of his own plans, the utter ignoring of personal responsibility toward his brother is the result.

All normal men crave the supernatural.

The supernatural realm was man's original realm; here, he reigned as king.

Sin came, and he was dethroned; yet all through human history we see the outreaching of man for the miraculous.

Satan has offered man many substitutes but all have been disappointing.

The Spirit Should Rule

When God created man, He planned that man's spirit should be the dominant reigning force.

Sin dethroned the spirit and made the body or mind dominant.

Humanity is divided between those whose minds rule the body and spirit, and those whose bodies rule the mind and spirit.

Among the great leaders in the educational, financial and social world, the mind is dominant.

Among another large portion in our land, the physical is dominant.

A generation ago we taught the boy and girl that they must keep the body under or it would destroy them.

Today, in our high schools, the physical has gained the ascendancy.

Christianity would restore the spirit to the place of dominance, if it had the opportunity.

Man must have food for his spiritual nature.

Man's spiritual nature must be exercised, developed, cultured, until it gains the ascendancy over the intellectual and physical.

When this becomes a reality, man shrinks from lawlessness.

This awakening of man's spiritual nature gives us our moral consciousness; it develops in us a responsibility toward our fellow man.

For a man to be educated mentally is to be one-third educated; to be educated physically and mentally is to be two-thirds educated; but to be educated mentally, physically, and spiritually is a well rounded education.

The Why of Bolshevism

To leave out the spiritual and magnify the mental makes man an anarchist—an unbalanced, ungoverned, and dangerous force in the world.

Take the supernatural out of Christianity and its flavor is gone; the element that makes it attractive to youth is eliminated.

Christianity must have a living God in it—One Who rules and demands a certain sacrifice, for religion without self-denial will fail.

Through all the ages, it has been a battle of the supernatural versus the intellectual.

The God of miracles is the God of the human, and when you eliminate the miraculous, you take away the attractive element of Christianity.

Chapter XVI

FELLOWSHIP AND RELATIONSHIP

OD is faithful, by whom you were called into the fellowship of Jesus Christ our Lord." 1 Cor. 1:9.

The entire plan of Redemption heads up in this wonderful word, "Fellowship," for what would Redemption and a New Creation mean if He had no fellowship with His Children.

The secrets of the Lord are with those who are in fellowship with Him.

The reason why "Believers" are unable to get into the Word and enjoy the fruit and privileges in Christ is because their fellowship is either broken or they have a very low type of fellowship.

The happiness of the home is in the fellowship between the members of that household. The real fruit of life is fellowship.

There would never be a divorce if fellowship had not been broken by the husband and wife.

When they are in fellowship, they desire children. When they are out of fellowship, they shrink from the very thought of it.

When fellowship is broken, they simply live together; they endure each other.

The desire for fellowship is the reason for marriage, and the joy of fellowship is the fruitage of marriage.

When one is born again and becomes a New Creation, the highest joy that the spirit has ever known comes from his fellowship with the Father and with Jesus and the Word.

The thing that breaks fellowship in the home is the thoughtless act and unkind word or look. It wounds the heart, it bruises the spiritual nature.

Fellowship is not a mental thing; it is spiritual. The mind comes into harmony with the spirit and enriches the fellowship.

When fellowship is broken with the Lord, the Bible becomes a closed book and it only condemns and hurts.

That is the reason that people who are out of fellowship have no appetite for the Word. They have no desire for prayer. They cannot use the Name of Jesus with any degree of felicity or joy. Their spirit nature is benumbed just like a paralyzed hand.

The Spirit says, "That which we have seen declare we unto you, that ye may have fellowship with us; and truly our fellowship is with the Father and with His Son, Jesus Christ.

These things write I unto you that your joy may be made full." (1 John 1:3-4).

Do you understand the difference between "happiness" and "joy?"

Happiness comes from right association. Joy comes from fellowship with the Father through the Word.

It is a strange, sweet experience, having prayer answered, to know that in the Name of Jesus you can cast out demons, you can set men free. You can bring joy to the heart of the Father and joy to your own heart.

"If we say that we have fellowship with Him and walk in darkness, we lie and do not the truth, but if we walk in the light, as He is in the light, we have fellowship one with another, and the blood of Jesus Christ His Son cleanseth us from all sin."

Our fellowship is threefold; with the Father, with the Word and with one another and I might also add with our own selves.

When your fellowship is broken, you know that you have lost something and you quarrel with your own mind and accuse yourself of having done something to break your fellowship and to forfeit your joy.

If we are so unwise to say that we have not sinned or done anything to break our fellowship, we are telling an untruth for the Father never withdraws his fellowship from anyone who is walking in the light. (1 John 2:8-9.)

"He that sayeth that he is in the light and hateth his brother is in darkness until now. He that loveth his brother abideth in the light and there is none occasion of stumbling in him, but the man who walks in darkness knows not where he is going." (His spirit is in darkness.)

But 1 John 1:9, "If we confess our sins, he is faithful and just or righteous to forgive us our sins and to cleanse us from all unrighteousness."

In 1 John 2:1, "These things write I unto you, that ye sin not, and if any man sin, we have an advocate with the Father, Jesus Christ the righteous."

The moment that you break fellowship, you should say "Father, in Jesus' name, forgive," and your Advocate or Lawyer seated at the right hand of the Father takes up your case and restores your broken fellowship.

It is not safe to be out of fellowship a moment, for when you are out of fellowship, you are in Satan's fellowship, without protection. You see that you are in the darkness and you cannot make wise decisions, you cannot get His Will.

You will never be led into false teaching as long as you are in fellowship with Him.

When you break your fellowship; it does not mean that you have broken your relationship; you are still his son. He alone can break your relationship. You alone can break your fellowship.

It is of vital importance that you know this lesson and walk in the light of it, for you never know when you will need the ability to approach the Father without fear for yourself or for some loved one, so walk in the light as He is in the light.

No one can use the Name while out of Fellowship, it is vitally important that one keep in the fullest fellowship every moment.

Chapter XVII

OUR SPIRITUAL INITIATIVE IN PRAYER

HE hindrance to our spiritual initiative in prayer comes from the neglect of reading and feeding on the Word. It is evidence of a low type of spiritual fellowship.

When we lose our spiritual initiative, we lose something that would drive us through to victory in hard places. It is time then that we should give ourselves to the study of the Word. It is the personal study of the Word that counts.

Whenever your faith loses its aggressiveness, the senses have gained the ascendancy.

Whenever spiritual things take second place, it is evidence that the realities of the divine things are losing out, that sense knowledge is slowly but surely gaining the mastery. It dominates at the "crossroads" where it is necessary that we have keen spiritual discernment. We cannot take a negative attitude toward the Word.

We assent to the Word instead of acting upon it. That holy fearlessness is lost.

The heart will not be saying, "I can do all things in Him today."

When the spiritual initiative is low, you will never hear one say, "Greater is He that is in me than the forces that surround me."

It is when the great things of Scripture are held as doctrines rather than as a reality, when the opinions of men are put above the Word of God. Out of this will grow an inferiority complex in the spiritual realm.

Whenever your heart loses its boldness towards the Lord, its fearlessness in acting on the Word, you are in danger. The prayer life has lost its reality and things of the senses have taken its place.

You see that is a real spiritual disease. Now the body becomes helpless. The mind where disease and fear grow and mature is under the dominion of an outside power and you are in a dangerous condition.

The cure is going to the Word again; giving yourself over to it, resolutely taking your place. Refuse to give up your confession.

Your Responsibility

We have seen the marvelous possibilities that belong to the believer who knows the authority and power that is invested in the Name of Jesus, and this knowledge carries with it a responsibility that cannot be ignored. You can never be the same kind of a Christian that you have been in the past.

You have caught a glimpse of what you might do if you dared to use the authority that is now your own, because the moment that you are recreated, that Name became yours. It gives you an opportunity to help those about you.

Most of us have been brought up to court our weaknesses and failings and to think of our lack of ability.

But there are sick and needy ones that could be helped through that Name. There are those bound by habits whom Satan rules with a merciless hand that could be set free if you would take your place.

I want you to notice the distinction between John 14:13-14 and John 16:23-24. "And whatsoever ye shall ask in my name, that will I do, that the Father may be glorified in the Son. If ye shall ask anything in my name, I will do it."

With this, goes Mark 16:17-20.

"He that believeth and is baptized shall be saved. He that disbelieveth shall be condemned. These signs shall accompany them that believe: In My Name, they shall cast out demons; they shall speak with new tongues; they shall take up serpents; if they shall drink any deadly thing, it shall in no wise hurt them; they shall lay hands on the sick and they shall recover.

"And they went forth and preached everywhere, the Lord working with them and confirming the word by the signs that followed."

Notice carefully, this Scripture differs from John 16:23-24 where Jesus says, "And in that day ye shall not pray to me. Verily, verily, I say unto you, if ye shall ask anything of the Father, He will give it you in my name; ask and ye shall receive that your joy may be made full."

In this Scripture, you are praying to the Father in Jesus' Name. In your praises and petitions, you come to the Father in Jesus' Name.

In the other Scripture, you are not praying, but you are using the authority of the Name to heal the sick, to cast out demons and to set men and women free.

Acts 3:1-10 illustrates this. Peter did not pray when he said to the impotent man, "in the name of Jesus Christ of Nazareth, walk."

There is no record of their praying for the sick in the book of Acts. They simply laid hands on them and commanded the adversary to leave and for the sick to arise and walk.

From Mark 16, you can see that the moment a man is born again he is expected to begin to use that Name. You lay your hands on the sick and say, "Disease leave this body."

Another staggering fact was that the Name was used largely in healing men and women who were not Christians. It evidently was God's method of advertising the ministry. So you can lay hands on the unsaved.

When you realize that this authority has been given to the individual members of the body of Christ and not to the ministry alone, it puts the responsibility squarely upon every believer. You are not only a member of the body, but you have become a responsible member of that body.

Another significant fact is that the word "Faith" or "Believe" does not occur in these Scriptures from the gospel of John. It is evident that the Believer had a legal right to the use of the Name and it was not a problem of Faith, but obedience to use the ability that God had given.

LAST WORDS

You have read this remarkable book. Many think it one of the most outstanding messages that has been given to the Church in the last fifty years. What is your responsibility after having read it? Should you not help us to give this message to the men and women who need it so desperately.

This book has changed the prayer life and the thinking of hundreds of thousands of people. The first ten thousand edition is said to have changed the prayer life of the whole Pacific Coast wherever this truth has gone.

The book has been translated into Chinese and has had a mighty ministry there.

Would it not be possible for you to invite some of your friends into your home and start a Bible class, going through this book and reading it carefully with your Bible in your hands? You should also read it along with my other books. A list of my other books is found on the last page. These books will fit you to teach the Word in such a way that you may become a blessing to the world.

If one understands what is written in this book, he need never live a life of defeat.

Write to us what your reactions are and if you would like to help us distribute this kind of literature.

You should read "The Father and His Family," a book, which reveals a true conception of our Redemption.

Inspiring Books
by E. W. KENYON

THE BIBLE IN THE LIGHT
OF OUR REDEMPTION
   A Basic Bible Course

ADVANCED BIBLE COURSE
   Studies in the Deeper Life

THE HIDDEN MAN OF THE HEART

WHAT HAPPENED
   From the Cross to the Throne

NEW CREATIONS REALITIES

IN HIS PRESENCE
   The Secret of Prayer

THE TWO KINDS OF LIFE

THE FATHER AND HIS FAMILY
   The Story of Man's Redemption

THE WONDERFUL NAME OF JESUS
   Our Rights and Privileges in Prayer

JESUS THE HEALER
   Has Brought Healing to Thousands

KENYON'S LIVING POEMS

THE NEW KIND OF LOVE

THE TWO KINDS OF FAITH

THE TWO KINDS OF RIGHTEOUSNESS

THE BLOOD COVENANT

THE TWO KINDS OF KNOWLEDGE

SIGN POSTS ON THE ROAD TO SUCCESS

IDENTIFICATION

Order From:
KENYON'S GOSPEL PUBLISHING SOCIETY
P.O. Box 973, Lynnwood, Washington 98046